GW00381831

**Rely on Thomas Cook as your
travelling companion on your next trip
and benefit from our unique heritage.**

Thomas Cook **pocket** guides

ROME

Thomas
Cook

Written by Zoë Ross with assistance from Frances Folsom
Updated by Giovanna Dunmall

Published by Thomas Cook Publishing
A division of Thomas Cook Tour Operations Limited
Company registration no. 3772199 England
The Thomas Cook Business Park, 9 Coningsby Road,
Peterborough PE3 8SB, United Kingdom
Email: books@thomascook.com, Tel: +44 (0) 1733 416477
www.thomascookpublishing.com

Produced by Cambridge Publishing Management Limited
Burr Elm Court, Main Street, Caldecote CB23 7NU
www.cambridgepm.co.uk

ISBN: 978-1-84848-353-8

© 2007, 2009 Thomas Cook Publishing
This third edition © 2011 Thomas Cook Publishing
Text © Thomas Cook Publishing
Maps © Thomas Cook Publishing/PCGraphics (UK) Limited
Transport map © Communicarta Limited

Series Editor: Karen Beaulah
Production/DTP: Steven Collins

Printed and bound in Spain by GraphyCems

Cover photography © Peter Adams Photography Ltd/Alamy

CONTENTS

SYMBOLS KEY

The following symbols are used throughout this book:

ⓐ address **ⓣ** telephone **ⓕ** fax **ⓦ** website address **ⓔ** email
ⓛ opening times **ⓝ** public transport connections **ⓘ** important

The following symbols are used on the maps:

𝒊 information office		▮ point of interest
✈ airport		⦿ city
✚ hospital		◉ large town
🛡 police station		○ small town
🚍 bus station		═ motorway
🚉 railway station		─ main road
Ⓜ metro		─ minor road
✝ cathedral		─ railway
❶ numbers denote featured cafés & restaurants		

Hotels and restaurants are graded by approximate price as follows:
£ budget price **££** mid-range price **£££** expensive

▶ *San Carlo al Corso dominating Rome's impressive skyline*

INTRODUCING
Rome

Introduction

Few other cities in the world have such a wealth of historic beauty, preserving the wonders of one of the most fascinating ancient civilisations – hence its nickname, *la Città Eterna* ('Eternal City'). For 21st-century visitors, these historic treasures can now be admired in even greater glory, after a large majority of the monuments and statues were restored as part of the Millennium projects in 2000. By day, they draw you in like a living and breathing history book, as you imagine the ancient footsteps that once trod the path you now tread; by night, the artfully placed floodlights create a magical glow of a timeless fairyland.

Italy may not have been fully united nor Rome declared its capital until 1870, but with its central position the city has always been integral to this boot-shaped landscape. The one-time political centre of one of the world's most successful and important empires and the nucleus of the Christian Church since the reported arrival of St Peter in the 1st century AD, Rome's influence has never been disputed. But, as with many capital cities, it is often looked on with disdain by the rest of the country. Romans are generally considered to be lazy and somewhat rude, compared to, say, the cultured refinement of the Florentines or the Bolognese. Romans, however, would argue that, as citizens of this bustling and important metropolis, they have less time for the niceties of daily life.

None of this, however, should influence the visitor to one of Europe's most enchanting cities. You don't even have to be a history buff to marvel at all there is to offer – imagining the roar of the crowd in the Colosseum, the ancient trading cries in the Forum, the wealthy lifestyles in the Renaissance *palazzi*, as well as the modern-day hum of the ubiquitous Vespas still embracing *la dolce vita*.

An important thing to remember, however, is that in a city so rich in heritage you cannot possibly see it all in one visit. Even a month here would allow you only to experience the basics, and the Vatican City alone warrants several days' exploration. For the first-time visitor, focus on a few of the unmissables, then give sightseeing a break, sit back and relax. History aside, one of the greatest charms of Rome is an early evening drink in the charming Campo de' Fiori, or a stroll through the alleyways in Trastevere, strung with laundry overhead. *This* is Rome today, and it's as vibrant as it has always been.

◗ *Experience Rome's long history at the Colosseum*

When to go

There are no hard-and-fast rules about when you should visit
Rome – year-round it has something to offer any visitor. However,
July and August can be uncomfortably hot (see below), and the
latter month sees an exodus of locals; you might have more
space in which to discover the city, but you'll also be harder
pressed to find somewhere to have lunch or dinner! All in all,
spring and autumn are better times to visit (although avoid
Easter, unless you want to share the city with heaving masses)
as the weather then is generally dry, warm and sunny. Winter,
too, has its advantages in that you'll have far fewer queues to
get into the attractions.

    Whenever you visit, you must bring the right togs. Comfortable,
hard-wearing shoes are required (heels do not fare well on the
centre's cobblestoned streets). The easiest way to get from one
sight to another is usually on foot. Even in places such as the
Vatican Museums, you will be covering vast distances. In summer,
cotton and linen clothing will be the coolest options, but don't
forget a jacket or cardigan. Not only do the evenings get cool, but
underground sights such as catacombs can be alarmingly chilly
compared to the baking sun outside.

SEASONS & CLIMATE

In the height of summer, the city can get more than a little warm.
Temperatures in excess of 35°C (95°F) are not unknown, and the heat
can combine with humidity to make things quite unpleasant. Spring
and autumn are usually lovely and, apart from very occasional days
that see a sprinkling of snow, winters are not particularly cold
(though lately they have been blighted by excessive rainfall).

ANNUAL EVENTS

Romans love to party, and whether it's a national holiday, the start of another arts or music extravaganza, or simply an obscure saint's day, the chances are you'll come across some kind of *festa* (festival) or another. Furthermore, any holiday that falls midweek is an invitation to *fare il ponte* (literally 'do a bridge'), which means that an extra day or two before the weekend are also holidays. What follows are just a few of the hundreds of special events and festivals celebrated in the city throughout the year.

January

Epifania (Feast of the Epiphany) A day on which La Befana, a witch, is said to reward good children with presents and bad children with a lump of coal. 🕒 6 Jan

February–March

Carnevale The last fling before Lent. Children dress up in costumes, and parades are held around the city.

March–April

Settimana Santa & Pasqua (Holy Week & Easter) Tourists and pilgrims pour into Rome on the Saturday before Palm Sunday, filling St Peter's Square (Piazza San Pietro) for the open-air Mass. Holy Week brings numerous religious services, culminating with the Papal Address on Easter Sunday. On Pasquetta (Easter Monday), by tradition Romans *fuori porta* (head for the mountains and parks outside the city) to relax and feast on picnics of *uove sode* (hard-boiled eggs) and *salumi* (cured meats). Ⓝ Vatican: Bus: 23, 40, 62, 64, 115, 116, 271, 280; Tram: 2, 19; Metro: Ottaviano-San Pietro

▲ *Many festivals are held in Rome's historical buildings*

Settimana della Cultura (Cultural Heritage Week) All state-owned museums and the many fascinating archaeological sites throughout Rome are open to the public free of charge. ⓦ www.beniculturali.it
🕒 Mid-Apr

June–September
Estate Romana In addition to the innumerable independently run arts festivals that cram the summer calendar, there are many city-run cultural events under the banner of *Estate Romana* (Roman Summer). For three months open-air concerts, plays and ballet performances are staged in venues dotted around the city. Many of the *Estate Romana* events are free; check newspapers, online and tourist boards for details. ⓦ www.estateromana.comune.roma.it

September–December
RomaEuropa Festival Following on, almost indistinguishably, from *Estate Romana*, is this autumn avant-garde arts festival of music, dance and theatre. Buy tickets at the venues or online.
Ⓦ www.romaeuropa.net

December
Immacolata Concezione (Feast of the Immaculate Conception)
A member of the local fire brigade, overseen by the Pope, is raised on a hydraulic platform to lay a wreath at the feet of the statue of the Madonna (which stands on top of a great stone column in the Piazza di Spagna). 🕐 8 Dec

PUBLIC HOLIDAYS
Capodanno (New Year's Day) 1 Jan
Epifania (Epiphany) 6 Jan
Pasqua (Easter Sunday) 24 Apr 2011; 8 Apr 2012; 31 Mar 2013
Lunedì di Pasqua (Easter Monday) 25 Apr 2011; 9 Apr 2012;
   1 Apr 2013
Festa della Liberazione (Liberation Day) 25 Apr
Festa del Lavoro (Labour Day) 1 May
Festa della Repubblica (Anniversary of the Republic) 2 June
Ferragosto (Feast of the Assumption) 15 Aug
Tutti Santi (All Saints' Day) 1 Nov
**Immacolata Concezione (Feast of the Immaculate
   Conception)** 8 Dec
Natale (Christmas) 25 Dec
Santo Stefano (Boxing Day) 26 Dec

Easter

As the centre of the Roman Catholic Church the two weeks leading up to Easter are the busiest time of the year in Rome. Tens of thousands of pilgrims, and tourists who just want to enjoy the spectacle, flood the city, taking up every hotel room in the place.

Tickets for the Masses and events are free but need to be reserved in advance. Check the Vatican website (Ⓦ www.vatican.va) for details and ticketing information. It's possible to attend without a ticket, but you'll have to stand for long periods of time.

Maundy/Holy Thursday – morning

At a special Mass (the Chrismal Mass), held in St Peter's Basilica (Basilica di San Pietro, see page 99) at 09.30, the Pope blesses the holy oils. This is one of the best times to get a glimpse of the Pope.

● *Thousands come to hear the Pope's Address at St Peter's Basilica*

Maundy/Holy Thursday – evening

The Triduum (three-day period between Holy Thursday and Easter Sunday) officially begins with the Pope holding a Mass at 17.30 in the **Basilica di San Giovanni in Laterano** (❷ Piazza San Giovanni in Laterano 4) to commemorate the Last Supper.

Good Friday – afternoon

Mass is said in the Vatican Chapel of St Peter's at 17.00, during which St John's account of Christ's suffering and death (known as 'the Passion') is sung and all present may kiss the Cross.

Good Friday – evening

Starting at 21.15, the Pope leads a solemn torch-lit procession, the *Via Crucis* (Ways of the Cross), from the Colosseum (see page 60) to Palatine Hill, re-enacting the 14 Stations of the Cross from Jesus' death sentence to the placement of his body in the tomb. Like his predecessors, the Pope carries a large wooden cross and at every station stops and offers a brief prayer. At the final station he gives his liturgy.

Holy Saturday

At 21.00, in the Papal Chapel of St Peter's, the Pope conducts the Easter Vigil, commencing the five-week Easter season.

Easter Sunday

The Pope celebrates Mass in St Peter's Square (see page 99) before delivering the *Urbi et Orbi* (meaning 'blessings on the city and the world') benediction from the Central Loggia of St Peter's Basilica. This is one of the most important religious events in Rome. Arrive early to find a good viewing spot.

History

The most popular legend surrounding the foundation of Rome, but undoubtedly pure myth, is that it was established by the twin brothers Romulus and Remus. The product of a rape by Mars of a Vestal Virgin, the young twins were cast aside and left to fend for themselves until they were rescued by a she-wolf who nursed them into adulthood. As adults, however, they became rival leaders of the city they created in what is now the Palatine Hill area and Remus was eventually murdered by Romulus. The latter therefore gave the city its name and became the first of its seven kings in 753 BC.

Nobody knows where this legend originated, but in reality it was the Etruscans who established the city, as they did much of Italy, in the 8th or 9th century BC. The Palatine and Capitoline Hills were a strategic choice for its foundation, protected by the lofty location while also being able to utilise the water source of the River Tiber. Proof of their existence here has emerged in various guises – 9th-century BC huts have been excavated beneath Palatine Hill, while historical documents tell tales of an Etruscan king in the region, Tarquinius Priscus, who reigned from 616 BC.

Documents also show that in 509 BC the grandson of King Tarquinius raped Lucretia, the wife of Collatinus, a Roman. Traumatised by the event, Lucretia committed suicide, but not before craftily telling her husband and his friend Brutus what had happened. In anger, grief and vengeance Collatinus and Brutus led a rebellion against the Tarquins, overthrowing the Etruscan dynasty and eventually establishing the Roman Republic. It was not just the city that grew in size and wealth; over the ensuing centuries the Romans proved themselves successful in expelling all other tribes, including the Sabines and the Samnites, as well as the Etruscans.

Then, not content with a countrywide Republic, they cast their sights further afield, eventually governing much of Western Europe under the banner of the Roman Empire.

The secret of their success is manifold. They were superb military leaders (with Julius Caesar among the finest), and understood the importance of establishing cities wherever they conquered to ensure continued control. They were also great politicians and masters of construction. The Via Appia (Appian Way), begun in 312 BC, not only linked Rome with southern Italy, and thereby Greece, but also became the prototype for all future Roman roads. At the same time, the Aqua Appia was the first aqueduct, illustrating how to bring fresh water from the river to the city. The construction of ports allowed trade links to grow and prosper, while the concept of a central forum established a link between traders, citizens and leaders.

It couldn't last, however. When Emperor Constantine converted to Christianity and moved the empire's capital to Byzantium, Rome became susceptible to invading tribes such as the Goths and the Vandals, and by AD 476 the empire had fallen.

That was then. These days, Rome, or rather Vatican City, is the home of the Holy See, and the city's glory is of a somewhat different nature, but it's no less impressive: now it springs from the city's countless attractions and from its status as not only Europe's most glamorous capital but also the world centre of stylish living.

In May 2008 the city elected a right-wing mayor, Gianni Alemanno, who promised to be tough on crime. Alemanno has sharpened the focus of both the city and its citizens on increasing the already massive amount of money brought in by tourism. Despite the recession, *la vita* in Rome is still *dolce*.

Lifestyle

Elegant and suave, sipping coffee in outdoor cafés or lounging around on their scooters, Romans deeply love their city and city life. That love is not blind, however, and while they can wax lyrical about its historical, cultural and architectural wonders, they also lament its traffic congestion, high pollution levels (which have improved), high cost of living, demonstrators regularly blocking city squares, disruptions caused by the high security for visiting VIPs, wildcat transport strikes that bring the city to a grinding halt, roadworks and bumper-to-bumper tour buses to name a few. That said, ask a Roman if they would want to live anywhere else and they will look at you as if you had two heads.

The pace of life may be frantic, but there's never a dull moment. To an extent, clichéd images hold true: nuns dodge the traffic alongside mobile phone-toting businessmen, clad in Armani and sporting slicked-back hair. Impossibly handsome teenagers flirt with each other in market squares such as Campo de' Fiori, while considerably stouter *mammas* stock up on fresh fruit and veg. Expat writers and artists while away the afternoon at a café in the Trastevere quarter while in nearby alleyways local *ragazzi* try to find room to kick about their beloved footballs.

The city centre may appear to be almost entirely inhabited by tourists and their ubiquitous cameras – and to a large extent it is. But there are many other layers to Rome, found in the lesser-known districts. The city changes constantly. Formerly working class, Testaccio is now a trendy place to live, with upmarket cafés, *trattorie* and wine bars. The gritty and formerly industrial area of Ostiense is also home to many restaurants and a pulsating nightlife scene, and more recently the formerly downbeat inner-city area of Pigneto

Rome, southeast of Termini Station, has become an unlikely centre for gourmet Roman cuisine.

In recent years Rome has had a reputation as a gay and lesbian centre. However, remember that this is a very Catholic city, and male machismo is rife. Same-sex couples should avoid public displays of affection. Active gay/lesbian organisations in Rome are **Arcigay Roma ORA** (ⓦ www.arcigay.it/roma) and **Circolo Mario Mieli** (ⓦ www.mariomieli.org).

◗ *Wander along the Ponte Sisto over the River Tiber*

Culture

Rome's one and only official arts centre, the **Palazzo delle Esposizioni** (Ⓐ Via Nazionale 194 Ⓦ www.palaexpo.it), was built in the 19th century specifically to host art exhibitions, a role it still fulfils. Excellent exhibitions are held on three floors, and there's a cinema, bookshop, café and successful gourmet restaurant.

Major art exhibits have a spectacular venue in the **Scuderie del Quirinale** (Ⓐ Via XXIV Maggio 16 Ⓣ 06 696270 Ⓦ www.scuderiequirinale.it), the former stables of the Palazzo Pontifico sul Quirinale. Built in 1730, the building was beautifully renovated by the Italian architect Gae Aulenti (of Paris' Musée d'Orsay fame). The Scuderie houses impressive touring exhibitions.

For a slightly more avant-garde cultural experience, check out the Centri Sociali, non-profit, self-governing social centres set up in various disused buildings around the city. They're a tradition begun by left-wing students during the 1970s, and still stage off-the-wall concerts, plays, arthouse film screenings and much more. It's a youthful scene – places where the under-30s can come for a drink, a political debate, a simple meal and some hard-hitting entertainment, although some resemble little more than a glorified squat. If this is your thing, the daily newspaper *La Repubblica* will give details of event times and places.

A relatively recent addition to Rome's cultural scene is the **Parco della Musica** (Ⓐ Viale Pietro de Coubertin Ⓣ 06 80241281 Ⓦ www.auditorium.com), designed by Renzo Piano and opened in 2002. Its three concert halls of varying size as well as an outdoor amphitheatre have played host to a vast and distinguished list of performers as well as numerous greats of the classical scene.

⬥ *Enjoy an opera or ballet at the popular Teatro dell'Opera*

Although not on the scale of Milan's La Scala, the **Teatro dell'Opera di Roma** (🅰 Via Beniamino 1 ☏ 06 48160287 🆆 www.operaroma.it) has stellar performances by Rome's opera and ballet companies. The season runs from October to June. In July and early August, the opera house relocates to the **Baths of Caracalla**. The largest thermal baths in the world date from the 3rd century and were in use until the fall of the Roman Empire. The idea of staging opera here belonged to Mussolini, but by 1993 productions were shut down because the 5,000-strong audiences were damaging the ruins. Restoration work was undertaken, audience size was reduced to 2,000 and opera recommenced here in 2000.

Throughout summer, open-air performances are held in parks and archaeological sites. Information can be found at tourist offices and in local newspapers. See 🆆 www.inromenow.com, 🆆 www.wantedinrome.com and 🆆 www.2night.it for details, too.

● *St Peter's Square in Vatican City*

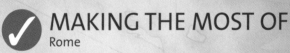 **MAKING THE MOST OF**
Rome

Shopping

Rome may be a bustling and hectic city, but shopping here is still remarkably quite a personalised experience. Some of the streets are pedestrianised, which means you can window-shop at leisure without keeping one eye out for traffic, and there is a wide range of markets that offer an authentic Italian experience. Rome has also retained a strong tradition of craftsmanship and there are many skilled artisans who take great pride in their work.

Most shops in the centre of Rome stay open all day. However, many, particularly in the outer districts, still observe traditional Italian hours: 15.30–19.30 Mon, 09.30–13.30, 15.30–19.30 Tues–Sat, closed on Sun. Food shops are often closed on Saturday afternoons in summer and Thursday afternoons in winter. Many shops close for at least two weeks between mid-July and mid-September.

The streets close to the Spanish Steps – Via Condotti, Via Borgognona and Via Frattina – are the ones to head for if you're after true Italian designer style, and designer prices. Here you'll find household names such as Gucci, Prada, Valentino, Bulgari, Versace and Armani. For those with a slightly lighter wallet, head to Via Nazionale, below Piazza della Repubblica, or Via Cola di Rienzo near the Vatican, where you'll still find plenty of style but with a more realistic price tag. The shops on and around Via del Corso will keep any teenager happy, while Via dei Giubbonari offers chic boutiques and hip designers. Via del Governo Vecchio offers a density of local fashion names.

If you're in the mood for antiques shopping, whether it be Renaissance furniture or retro 1960s Bakelite, head for Via dei Coronari, Via dell'Orso and Via dei Soldati, north of Piazza Navona. Another good source of art and antiques is Via Giulia and the area between Piazza del Popolo and the Spanish Steps. The largest flea market in Rome – and, some say, in Europe – is held every Sunday in Trastevere.

Rome abounds in food shops, but the best option is the markets around Campo de' Fiori or Via Cola di Rienzo across the river. These are always worth a visit for sheer street theatre.

USEFUL SHOPPING PHRASES

What time do the shops open/close?
A che ora aprono/chiudono i negozi?
Ah keh ohrah ahprohnoh/kewdohnoh ee nehgotsee?

How much is this?
Quanto costa questo?
Kwantoh kostah kwestoh?

Can I try this on?
Posso provarlo?
Pohsoh prohvarloh?

My size is ...
La mia taglia è ...
Lah meeyah tahlyah eh ...

I'll take this one, thank you
Prenderò questo, grazie
Prehndehroh kwestoh, grahtsyeh

Can you show me the one in the window/this one?
Può mostrarmi quello in vetrina/questo?
Poh mohstrahrmee kwehloh een vehtreenah/kwestoh?

This is too large/too small/too expensive
È troppo grande/troppo piccolo/troppo caro
Eh trohpoh grahndeh/trohpoh peekohloh/trohpoh kahroh

Eating & drinking

Italians as a whole are in love with food, so it's no surprise that the capital would also place cuisine very high on its agenda. In even the most modest of establishments, your food is likely to be the freshest that is available that day – Italians hold little sway with frozen meat or vegetables. Their insistence on quality is also shown by the amount of time they like to spend savouring the produce – even busy Romans will take hours out of their day to spend them eating and socialising over lunch or dinner.

In recent years the restaurant scene in Rome has also gone up a notch. As well as traditional *trattorie,* serving simple pasta and meat dishes, there are now trendy mozzarella bars, wine bars serving gourmet dishes and restaurants where you can listen to live music, eat and dance. Even the humble pizza has been given a new lease of life.

If you're not a fan of Italian cuisine, however, you're likely to go hungry. Italy, and by the same token Rome, is so proud of its own creations that it's never really felt the need to embrace other cultures on this front. There are, however, a few decent Chinese, Japanese and Indian restaurants.

One speciality in Rome that may not appeal to all tastes is the use of animal offal – the *quinto quarto,* or 'fifth quarter' parts of

PRICE CATEGORIES

The restaurant price guides used in the book indicate the approximate cost of a three-course meal for one person, excluding drinks, at the time of writing.

£ up to €25 ££ €25–55 £££ over €55

a beast that are left over after the prime cuts of meat are sold off. That means *cervello* (brains), *nervetti* (beef tendons), *coda* (oxtail), *pajata* (baby veal intestines) and *animelle* (the thymus glands in an animal's throat) can often be seen on menus. *Trattorie* in the neighbourhoods of Testaccio and Trastevere are known for these delicacies.

Vegetarians should have no problem in choosing a suitable option from any menu. Many pasta dishes and pizzas are made entirely without meat, and lentils and other pulses are a frequent offering. Fresh vegetables and cheeses are also plentiful.

Restaurants are generally open at 12.30–16.00, then again at 19.30–24.00, and some stay open later. A few are open through the day.

❶ Remember many restaurants close for at least three weeks in July or August. It's a good idea to make reservations in advance, particularly in high season, and at the weekend, when it's busier.

🔺 *Watch the world go by over a drink in Piazza di Pietra*

The typical Italian meal starts with *antipasti*, which are tapas-style bite-sized variations of cold cuts, seafood and vegetables. Next, *Il Primo* (first course) is usually a soup or pasta dish, followed by *Il Secondo* (second course), consisting of meat or fish. Italians rarely eat pasta as a main course, so portions are smaller than you would find in Italian restaurants abroad. Vegetables (*contorni*) are ordered separately, so don't assume your main course will come with an accompaniment unless you

USEFUL DINING PHRASES

I would like a table for ... people
Vorrei un tavolo per ... persone
Vohray oon tahvohloh pehr ... pehrsohneh

Excuse me!	**May I have the bill, please?**
Scusi!	Mi dà il conto, per favore?
Skoozhee!	*Mee dah eel cohntoh, pehr fahvohreh?*

Could I have it well cooked/medium/rare please?
Potrei averlo ben cotto/mediamente cotto/al sangue, per favore?
Pohtray ahvehrloh behn kohtoh/mehdyahmehnteh kohtoh/ ahl sahngweh, pehr fahvohreh?

I am a vegetarian. Does this contain meat?
Sono vegetariano/vegetariana (fem.). Contiene carne?
Sohnoh vehjehtaryahnoh/vehjehtaryahnah. Kontyehneh kahrneh?

TIPPING

A service charge of 10–15 per cent will sometimes be included, in which case no further tip is required. Restaurants are no longer allowed to add the *pane e coperto* (bread and cover charge) to the bill. However, most establishments blithely ignore this and charge it anyway. A tip of between 5 and 10 per cent of the bill is always adequate; Romans will often only leave a few euros in coins.

order them. The meal usually ends with *frutta* (fresh fruit) or a selection of *dolci* (sweet desserts), followed by coffee and a *digestivo* (liqueur). Five courses may seem like a lot, but remember that portion sizes reflect this, and no one will frown on you if you order less, as many now do. Few restaurants impose a strict dress code, although shorts and T-shirts are frowned upon in the more exclusive places.

Ask for *il conto* when you want the bill – but expect a bit of a wait. Romans are never in a hurry to leave the dining table and waiters are used to this attitude.

Children are welcome in Roman restaurants, even the posh ones. Usually *un seggiolone* (a high chair) is available on request, as is *una mezza porzione* (a half-portion).

Many of Rome's clubs are trendy places where the 'beautiful people' go to see and be seen. The *enoteca* or *vineria* (wine bar) has always been a favourite hangout in Rome. Most of them, particularly the newer ones, offer extensive wine lists and gourmet menus.

❶ Smoking is now illegal in all restaurants and bars.

Entertainment & nightlife

Everything you've ever thought about Italian style and posing becomes apparent when you walk through the door of Rome's more popular clubs. If you want cheaper prices and less fashion pressure, however, head for the smaller venues – you'll find details in local listings magazines. To beat the licensing laws, many of Rome's clubs are listed as private, which means they charge a membership fee just to enter, although this usually includes the price of a drink.

The best areas for nightlife can be found in Trastevere, the *centro storico* (around Piazza Navona in particular), Testaccio and Ostiense (to the southwest of Trastevere). Pick up a copy of *Roma C'È* (ⓦ www.romace.it), published every Wednesday and available from newsagents (approximately €1). Otherwise *TrovaRoma*, in *La Repubblica*'s Thursday edition, is another helpful guide. The fortnightly English-language *Wanted in Rome* magazine (ⓦ www.wantedinrome.com) lists events.

City-wide venues feature summer festivals of live music; July to early September welcomes the Jazz & Image Festival at the Villa Celimontana park (ⓦ www.villacelimontanajazz.com). November brings the **Roma Jazz Festival** (ⓦ www.romajazz.com), which attracts big-name musicians.

Latin music is gaining in popularity, so if you fancy a bit of salsa beat don't miss **Fiesta!** (ⓦ www.fiesta.it). The festival runs from mid-June to mid-August at the **Ippodromo delle Cappannelle** (ⓐ Via Appia Nuova 1245).

Other live music offerings in summer include the **Luglio suona bene** (ⓦ www.auditorium.com/lugliosuonabene) programme of jazz, pop and rock concerts (with international headliners) that takes place throughout the month of July in Parco della Musica (see page 18).

The **Cosmophonies** music festival (Ⓦ www.cosmophonies.com) hosts grand concerts in the amphitheatre of Ostia Antica (see page 125). Roma Incontra Il Mondo, a series of concerts with Italian and world music performers, takes place every year from mid-June to mid-August against the atmospheric backdrop of the **Villa Ada** park (Ⓦ www.villaada.org and Ⓦ www.estateromana.comune.roma.it).

⬤ *Romantic Rome by night*

Sport & relaxation

Rome was, of course, home to the crowd-jeering gladiatorial fights in ancient times, so it has a long tradition of providing spectator sports. The national sport, in fact obsession, is *calcio* (football) and during big matches you'll see most Romans glued to the small screen in bars and cafés. On the whole, sport is seen very much as something to watch rather than do – but these days there are more *palestre* (gyms) in town than ever before.

PARTICIPATION SPORTS
Cycling
The month of May brings the *Giro d'Italia* (Italy's national race), when competitive cyclists can be seen spinning through Rome's narrow cobbled streets. At any other time of the year, Rome's incessant traffic makes cycling a death-wish choice, but the Via Appia Antica is closed to automobiles, offering the chance to get on two wheels for a leisurely afternoon; there's a bike-hire outlet at the information point on Via Appia Antica 58 (🕐 09.30–13.30, 14.00–17.30 Mon–Sat, closed Sun).

SPECTATOR SPORTS
Football
Rome has two principal football teams, Roma and Lazio, both of which play at the **Stadio Olimpico** (🚊 Via Foro Italico, off Via dello Stadio Olimpico ☎ 06 3237333) on alternate Sundays from September to May. As a rule, Roma is the favourite of the left-wing working class while Lazio is the team of choice for the conservative populace. Rivalries run high and the sport can be quite violent, on and off the playing field. Stadio Olimpico seats around 82,000 for most games.

With the exception of Roma–Lazio clashes, tickets should be available on the day of the event.

Lazio supporters sit on the *Curva Nord* (North End) of the stadium waving their colours of blue and white, with the eagle as their symbol. Roma fans, whose symbol is the wolf and whose colours are blue and yellow, take over the *Curva Sud* (South End) of the stadium. If you attend a game, make sure you're cheering for the right team on the right side if you want to avoid any trouble.

For information in English about the season's games, go to the *Federazione Italiana Giuoco Calcio* (Ⓦ www.figc.it). Or if you read Italian, pick up the Rome paper *Corriere dello Sport*, which gives details of upcoming games.

Ticket prices vary from €15 to €100. They can be purchased from the following official club stores: AS Roma Store ⓐ Piazza Colonna 360 (near Piazza di Spagna) Ⓦ www.asroma.it; and Lazio Fan Shop ⓐ Via degli Scipioni 84 (near the Vatican) Ⓦ www.sslazio.it, or online Ⓦ www.ticketone.it or Ⓦ www.listicket.it

◯ *Fans prepare for a match at the Stadio Olimpico*

Accommodation

Rome has a vast range of hotel accommodation so even if you arrive in the city without a booking you're likely to be able to find a room. However, if you're travelling in high season (Easter to October and Christmas to New Year) it's best to book in advance, as it would be anywhere else.

If you want to find a room on arrival, your best bets are the Enjoy Rome office (see page 153) or the free hotel reservation service, with desks at Termini Station (opposite platform 20) and Fiumicino and Ciampino Airports. It has English-speaking staff and is open daily, 07.00–22.00 (you can also book online ⓦ www.rexervation.it).

HOTELS

The Beehive £ This light, bright and clean hotel offers a fetching garden and great rates near the station (there is one dorm room too). They also offer well-priced local apartments and are genuinely friendly and helpful. ⓐ Via Marghera 8 (Monti, Esquilino & Quirinale) ⓽ 06 44704553 ⓦ www.the-beehive.com ⓝ Metro: Termini

Cervia £ A wonderful-value *pensione* given its location right in the city centre. All rooms have private baths. The top-floor rooms

> #### PRICE CATEGORIES
> The ratings in this book are for a double room for one night in high season (including VAT and breakfast).
> **£** up to €110 **££** €110–220 **£££** over €220

are cheaper because there's no lift. ⊖ Via Palestro 55 (Monti, Esquilino & Quirinale) ❶ 06 491057 ⓦ www.hotelcerviaroma.com Ⓝ Bus: 16, 36, 75, 90, 92, 204, 217, 310, 360, 492, 649; Metro: Castro Pretorio

Aphrodite ££ This 3-star hotel, located next to Termini Station, not only offers comfortable en-suite rooms but also benefits from a roof terrace, which is a godsend in the summer. ⊖ Via Marsala 90 (Monti, Esquilino & Quirinale) ❶ 06 491096 ⓦ www.aphroditehotelrome.com Ⓝ Metro: Termini

Daphne Inn ££ A boutique hotel for those on a budget, the Daphne has two locations off Piazza Barberini. Rooms are large and stylish with free Wi-Fi, but what sets this place apart is its excellent service and the staff's useful travel tips and advice; they even give you a local mobile phone to use during your visit. (There is no lift at the Daphne Trevi location.) ⊖ Via degli Avignonesi 20 and Via di San Basilio 55 (Monti, Esquilino & Quirinale) ❶ 06 87450086 ⓦ www.daphne-rome.com Ⓝ Bus: 52, 53, 61, 62, 63, 80, 95, 116, 119, 175, 492, 630; Metro: Barberini

Gerber ££ Comfortable and pleasant and very conveniently situated between Villa Borghese and St Peter's, ideal for sightseeing. Rates include breakfast and taxes. ⊖ Via degli Scipioni 241 (Vatican City) ❶ 06 3216485 ⓦ www.hotelgerber.it Ⓝ Bus: 30, 70, 130, 186, 224, 280, 590, 913; Metro: Lepanto

Isa ££ This boutique hotel is in the elegant Prati district, between the Vatican and the Spanish Steps. All rooms are en-suite and there's a romantic roof garden. ⊖ Via Cicerone 39 (Vatican City)

⬤ *A plain entrance leads to boutique-hotel heaven*

☎ 06 3212610 🌐 www.hotelisa.net 🚍 Bus: 30, 70, 186, 280, 590, 913;
Metro: Lepanto

Lancelot ££–£££ This hotel has elegant rooms, some of them with
terraces. The only suite has a flower-filled terrace overlooking the
Colosseum and there's an internal courtyard where guests can have
breakfast. Visitors rave about this old-world hotel and its regular
'roundtable dinners' that guests are invited to attend. 📍 Via Capo
d'Africa 47 ☎ 06 70450615 🌐 www.lancelothotel.com 🚍 Bus: 87, 571;
Tram: 3; Metro: Colosseo

Locarno ££–£££ Filled with appealing Art Deco touches, the Locarno's
rooms and luxury suites (all situated in a new wing) are decorated
with discreet antiques and Art Deco-style wallpaper and fabrics. The
chic boutiques and restaurants of the Piazza di Spagna area are just
round the corner. The hotel does a generous buffet breakfast, which
is served on the roof-garden terrace in summer. 📍 Via della Penna 22
☎ 06 3610841 🌐 www.hotellocarno.com 🚍 Bus: 81, 95, 117, 119, 224, 590,
628, 913, 926; Tram: 2; Metro: Flaminio

Aleph £££ A boutique hotel with a glamorous lobby, a buzzing bar
and restaurant, bedrooms with 1930s- and 1940s-inspired furniture,
and a beautiful spa with a mosaic spa downstairs. 📍 Via San
Basilio 15 (Monti, Esquilino & Quirinale) ☎ 06 422901
🌐 www.boscolohotels.com 🚍 Bus: 61, 62, 116, 150, 175, 492, 590;
Metro: Barberini

Portrait Suites £££ This apartment-style boutique hotel in Rome's
high-fashion neighbourhood is a sophisticated outpost of the
Salvatore Ferragamo fashion empire. The rooftop terrace alone

is worth the money; it offers one of the most sumptuous views of the city.  Via Bocca di Leone 23 (Via del Corso & Tridente) 06 69380742 www.lungarnohotels.com Bus: 116, 117, 119, 590; Metro: Spagna

St George Roma £££ The St George is a great little contemporary hotel right in the heart of Rome, on a beautiful, elegant cobbled street a short walk away from the bustling Campo de' Fiori and St Peter's. There's a spa and restaurant, too. Via Giulia 62 (*centro storico*) 06 686611 www.stgeorgehotel.it Bus: 23, 40, 46, 64, 116, 271, 280, 571, 916

HOSTELS

Alessandro Hostels £ These two hostels have been voted among the top ten in Europe, so understandably they're always crowded. Book in advance. The Palace Alessandro has en-suite baths in every room, unusual for hostel accommodation, while the Downtown Alessandro has dormitory rooms and shared baths. Amenities at both include breakfast, Internet access, free soft drinks and regular pasta and pizza parties. Both are a ten-minute walk from Termini Station.

Alessandro Palace Hostel Via Vicenza 42 (Monti, Esquilino & Quirinale) 06 4461958 www.hostelalessandropalace.com Metro: Termini

Alessandro Downtown Hostel Via C Cattaneo 23 (Monti, Esquilino & Quirinale) 06 44340147 www.hostelalessandrodowntown.com Metro: Termini

CAMPSITES

Understandably Rome's campsites are located outside the city, so bear in mind travelling time when booking.

Camping Tiber £ Spacious and friendly, with swimming pool and hot showers. Free shuttle service to and from nearby Prima Porta Station. ⓐ Via Tiberina, KM 1,400 ❶ 06 33610733 ⓦ www.campingtiber.com ⓜ Metro: from Termini Station take the A line to the Flaminio stop. From there take the Roma–Viterbo train to the Prima Porta stop and then take the shuttle bus to the campsite.

Flaminio Village £ Modern facilities, swimming pool and the closest site to the city centre. ⓐ Via Flaminia Nuova 821 ❶ 06 3332604 ⓦ www.villageflaminio.it ⓜ From Termini Station, take metro line A to Flaminio. From there take the local train to Prima Porta, alighting at Due Ponti.

SELF-CATERING

Rome is one of the best cities in which to rent a holiday apartment, and it offers both a good-value option and a more personalised feel than a hotel. All the places listed here have websites offering pictures of the accommodation. Also check out the biweekly magazine *Wanted in Rome* (see page 28).

City Apartments ❶ 06 978 45999 ⓦ www.cityapartments.it

Enjoy Rome ⓐ Via Marghera 8a ❶ 06 445 1843 ⓦ www.enjoyrome.com

Landmark Trust Apartment overlooking the Spanish Steps. Sleeps four. ⓐ Piazza di Spagna ❶ UK (01628) 825 925 ⓦ www.landmarktrust.org.uk

Rome Sweet Home ⓐ Via delle Vite 32 ❶ 06 699 24833 ⓦ www.romesweethome.com

THE BEST OF ROME

So many sights, so little time. The best thing to do in Rome is to enjoy the city at an easy pace; you're never going to be able to see it all in just one visit, and even if you do you'll end up history-lagged. Pick and choose what interests you the most and let the beauty of what you see sink in. Then throw a coin in the Trevi Fountain, which will ensure you return.

TOP 10 ATTRACTIONS

- **Vatican City and Basilica di San Pietro (St Peter's Basilica)** An independent and sovereign state with the principal shrine of the Catholic Church (see page 99).

- **Piazza Navona** Rome's most famous square is busy and full of life from dawn until late (see page 86).

- **Scalinata di Trinità dei Monti (Spanish Steps)** A stunning set of steps that has a truly intriguing history (see page 92).

- **Foro Romano (Roman Forum)** The centre of Ancient Rome and thus the one-time centre of the world (see page 63).

- **Il Campidoglio (Capitoline Hill)** The political hub of the Roman Empire (see page 58).

- **Pantheon** A magnificent feat of architecture (see page 85).

- **Monumento a Vittorio Emanuele II (Monument to Vittorio Emanuele II)** This awe-inspiring building gives panoramic views of the city (see page 72).

- **Colosseo (Colosseum)** The largest amphitheatre in the Roman Empire witnessed many a gladiatorial epic (see page 60).

- **Fontana di Trevi (Trevi Fountain)** Magnificent Baroque fountain of iconic significance (see page 109).

- **Cappella Sistina (Sistine Chapel)** Priceless artwork made glorious by the genius of Michelangelo (see page 104).

🔽 St Peter's Square is the place to congregate

Suggested itineraries

HALF-DAY: ROME IN A HURRY

Head to the Roman Forum (see page 63) to get a sense of what life was like during the Roman Republic. This was home to political and religious institutions, shops and markets, and remained the most important area until the Republic became an empire in 50 BC and Julius Caesar built the Imperial Fora (see page 60) nearby.

1 DAY: TIME TO SEE A LITTLE MORE

Continue the Ancient Rome itinerary with the Palatine Hill and the Colosseum (see page 60). At the bottom of the hill turn right at the Arch of Titus to get to the main entrance of the Colosseum. Clinging to the side of the hill are the ruins of the Baths of Septimius Severus.

One of the crown jewels in Rome's ancient monuments is the Colosseum. Awe-inspiring, it needs little historical knowledge to explain its function. Imagine the clanging of the gladiators, cries of the Christians and the roar of the crowds. After each battle or sacrifice sand was thrown on the arena floor to soak up the blood. To avoid the crowds visit in the early morning or late afternoon.

2–3 DAYS: TIME TO SEE MUCH MORE

Walk behind the Pantheon (see page 85) to Piazza della Minerva and you will find Bernini's diminutive and whimsical *Elephant* statue. The obelisk on the elephant's back is a reference to the reign of Pope Alexander VII, to illustrate the fact that strength supports wisdom. In front of you is the grand façade of **Santa Maria sopra Minerva** (❶ 06 6793926), the only Gothic church in Rome, built in the late 13th century over the ruins of a temple to Minerva. Inside is the Carafa Chapel with its fresco of *The Assumption* by Filippino Lippi and, on the left side of the altar, Michelangelo's *Christ Bearing the Cross*, c. 1521.

The Fontana di Trevi (Trevi Fountain) and the Spanish Steps (see page 92) have been drawing tourists since the 18th century when Rome was on the itinerary of the Grand Tour. The Trevi Fountain was begun by Salvi in 1732 and finished in 1762 by Pannini. It is a massive Baroque creation: Neptune stands in a shell chariot pulled by horses in front of a triumphal arch (see also page 109).

A good place to find some shade on a sweltering summer day is the **Villa Borghese**, a series of parks that form the core of Rome's largest central open space. Made up of the grounds of the 17th-century *palazzo* of Cardinal Scipione Borghese, it's a huge area, with a boating lake, a zoo and three of the city's finest museums.

The Piazza Navona (see page 86) is crowded day and night with tourists, street musicians, buskers and artists. Hang out at the fountains or do as some locals do, and take your evening stroll (or *passeggiata*) here.

LONGER: ENJOYING ROME TO THE FULL

Allow several days to explore the Vatican (see page 99); Castel Sant'Angelo, St Peter's Basilica, the gardens, galleries and museums all make up the richest but most exhausting museum complex in the world.

The Sistine Chapel (see page 104), a barn-like structure built between 1473 and 1481 for Pope Sixtus IV, is the Pope's private chapel. The ceiling and wall murals here are regarded by many as the greatest masterpieces in Western art executed by one man, Michelangelo. An average day brings in excess of 20,000 visitors to the chapel.

Something for nothing

Rome can be as expensive or inexpensive as you want it to be. In fact the cheapest and most enjoyable pastime in Rome is simply walking around the city's piazzas, parks, outdoor artwork, monuments, fountains, ancient architecture and colourful gardens.

Many churches, particularly those located in out-of-the-way neighbourhoods, are free, offering a splendid chance to see beautiful interiors and liturgical artwork.

During *Settimana della Cultura* (Cultural Heritage Week, see page 10) state-owned museums throughout Rome are open to the public at no charge. In mid-May there is also the annual *Notte dei Musei*, a Saturday night when museums, galleries and archaeological sites are open for free from 20.00 to 02.00.

The Vatican Museums offer free admission on the last Sunday of the month.

From June to September there are free performances of music, dance and opera at many of the city's open parks and squares.

At the *aperitivo* hour, wine bars and cafés put out tempting food samplings, so dust off your backpacks, change your clothes and join the foray – for the price of a drink you can dine well.

Or, when in Rome do as the Romans do and simply people-watch from an outdoor café or the steps of an ancient church.

⬥ *The 4th-century San Sebastiano church has a rich history*

When it rains

There's no need to let the odd shower dampen your enthusiasm for this glorious city. Your rainy-day options could well include some of the imperial city's more intriguing possibilities.

The **Catacombe di San Callisto** (Catacomb of St Callixtus ⓐ Via Appia Antica 110–126 ⓣ 06 51301580 ⓦ www.catacombe.roma.it) is a splendidly creepy idea. Rome has many catacombs (underground burial vaults), but these are the largest; they house the remains of St Callixtus, and other early popes are buried here in the papal crypt. Some of the walls are also decorated with frescoes.

Down the road from St Callixtus, in a basilica built by Emperor Constantine, are the **Catacombe di San Sebastiano** (Catacombs of St Sebastian ⓐ Via Appia Antica 136 ⓣ 06 7850350 ⓦ www.catacombe.org). It is believed that the remains of Saints Peter and Paul were hidden here to protect them from the vile intentions of body snatchers until they could be moved on to their final resting places. A statue of St Sebastian adorns his tomb, and opposite this is a slab of marble that is allegedly imprinted with the footprints of Christ. The walls contain paintings of doves and fish, which were symbols of Christianity in early times.

An invaluable addition to Rome's arts scene was the opening of the **MAXXI Museo Nazionale delle Arti del XXI Secolo** (National Museum of the 21st Century Arts) in May 2010 after an 11-year construction period. This stunning building, located in the northern Flaminio district, just across from the music auditorium, was designed by Anglo-Iraqi architect Zaha Hadid. The museum is dedicated to 20th-century and contemporary art and architecture, as well as providing all-important temporary exhibition space. ⓐ Via Guido Reni 4a ⓣ 06 39967350 ⓦ www.fondazionemaxxi.it

🕐 11.00–19.00 Tues, Wed & Fri–Sun, 11.00–22.00 Thur, closed Mon
🚌 Bus: 53, 200, 217, 220, 233, 446, 910; Tram: 2 ℹ Admission charge

Less high-profile, but also providing a much-needed injection into Rome's arts and architecture scene, is **MACRO Museo d'Arte Contemporanea di Roma** (Rome's Contemporary Art Museum), located not far from Piazza Fiume in a converted former Peroni brewery. The venue, which saw the creation of a new wing and a vast rooftop area-cum-garden housing a café and terrace that opened in late 2010, was expanded under a project by French architect Odile Decq. The venue pulls in big international names as well as young and local artists. Some shows are also displayed at another venue – MACRO Future – in the former slaughterhouse in Testaccio (📍 Piazza Orazio Giustiniani 4 🕐 16.00–24.00 Tues–Sun, closed Mon), which is only open when there's an exhibition. 📍 Via Reggio Emilia 54 ☎ 06 671070400 🌐 www.macro.roma.museum 🕐 09.00–19.00 Tues–Sun, closed Mon 🚌 Bus: 38, 62, 80, 88, 90 ℹ Admission charge

🔺 The stunning MAXXI museum

On arrival

Air and train are the best ways to arrive in Rome. Arrival by car can be stressful during rush-hour traffic.

TIME DIFFERENCE
Italy is on Central European Time (CET). During Daylight Saving Time (late Mar–late Oct), clocks are set one hour ahead.

ARRIVING
By air
Rome is serviced by two airports. Leonardo da Vinci International, known as Fiumicino, is located 36 km (22 miles) southwest of the city and handles most scheduled flights. Ciampino, 16 km (10 miles) southeast of Rome, is the airport of choice for both charter and budget airlines. **Aeroporti di Roma** (Ⓦ www.adr.it) provides live flight information for both airports and timetables in English.

There are three terminals at Fiumicino Airport: A for domestic flights, B for international flights within the EU, and C for all other international flights. The airport is connected to the city by trains to Termini Station, which take 30 minutes. They cost €14, and the service begins at 06.37, leaving every half-hour until 23.37. A slightly cheaper option (€8) is to take a train to Trastevere, then take tram No 8 into the city centre.

The city's second aiport, Ciampino Airport, does not have a rail connection. If you arrive on one of the budget airlines, take their shuttle bus that leaves 30 minutes after each arrival for Termini Station. Another option is the COTRAL buses that run every 30 minutes from the airport to the Anagnina metro station, at the end of metro line A. The 30-minute trip costs about €1.20, and from there it's a 20-minute metro ride into the city, which costs €1.

Taxis are the most convenient but most expensive way of getting to and from the airport. In 2006 the city authorities introduced fixed taxi fares of €40 and €30 (respectively) – including luggage and up to four people – between Fiumicino and Ciampino Airports and the city centre. (Make sure you mention this before you get in the taxi as scams are common at the airport.)

◯ The city's 19th-century aquarium now houses an architectural cultural centre

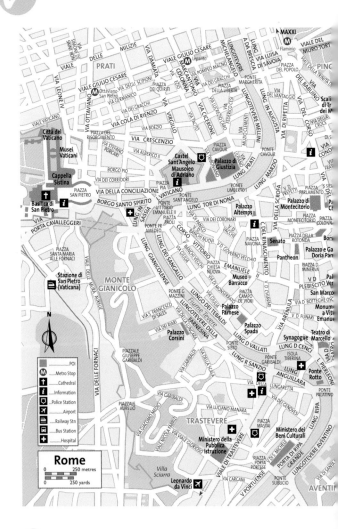

Rome

0 ——— 250 metres
0 ——— 250 yards

- POI
- Ⓜ Metro Stop
- Cathedral
- i Information
- Police Station
- Airport
- Railway Stn
- Bus Station
- Hospital

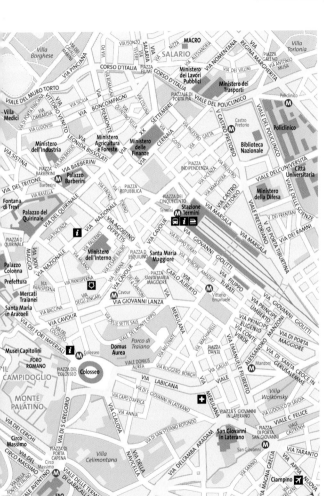

49

By rail

Stazione Termini (② Piazza dei Cinquecento) – more commonly known as Termini – is the main railway station in Rome, and the one at which you are likely to arrive when travelling by train to Rome. Both metro lines pass through and many of the bus routes terminate here. Termini has a left-luggage department, which is open 06.00–24.00 and costs about €4 per item per five hours. For train timetables and information on prices and connections from any station in Italy, call ① 892021 from a land line or mobile phone (in Italy), or log on to ⓦ www.ferroviedellostato.it (tickets can be bought online with a credit card).

By road

There are numerous bus stations in Rome, but the main ones are outside the following metro stations: Lepanto, Ponte Mammolo and Tiburtina (for routes north), and Anagnina and EUR Fermi (for routes south).

Driving into Rome is not recommended – the traffic is manic and parking in the city is a continual nightmare. However, if you must drive, then follow these instructions: if coming from the north on the A1 motorway, take the Roma Nord exit, and if coming from the south, take the Roma Est exit. Both routes culminate at the Grande Raccordo Anulare (GRA) road, which runs around the city and connects all the major routes into Rome's city centre. From Ciampino, follow Via Appia Nuova into the centre, or join the GRA at junction 23 and follow the signs to the centre. From Fiumicino take the A12 motorway into the city centre; this route crosses the river just north of the suburb EUR. From there it is a short drive north up Via Cristoforo Colombo to the city walls, and beyond to the Baths of Caracalla.

IF YOU GET LOST, TRY ...

Excuse me, do you speak English?
Mi scusi, parla inglese?
Mee skoozee, pahrleh eenglehzeh?

Excuse me, is this the right way to Via .../the city centre/the tourist office/the station/the bus station?
Mi scusi, questa è la strada giusta per Via .../il centro/l'ufficio informazioni turistiche/la stazione ferroviaria/la stazione degli autobus?
Mee skoozee, kwestah eh lah strahdah justah pehr Veeyah .../ eel chentroh/loofeecho eenfohrmahtsyonee tooreesteekeh/ lah stahtsyoneh fehrohveeahreeah/lah stahtsyoneh dehlyee owtohboos?

ORIENTATION

Rome's city centre is divided into blocks. The web of streets making up the *centro storico* (historic centre) occupies a spit of land on the left bank of the River Tiber, bordered on the east by Via del Corso and the north and south by water. Spreading east from here is Rome's central core, across the Via del Corso to the major shopping streets and alleyways that surround the Spanish Steps, down to Via Nazionale and beyond to the ancient city in the south and to Villa Borghese park to the north. The left bank of the river is home to the Vatican and St Peter's, while to the south of these is the buzzy and charming neighbourhood of Trastevere. It can be quite easy to lose your way, particularly if you head down the many alleyways that entice with sounds and smells, so always carry a map.

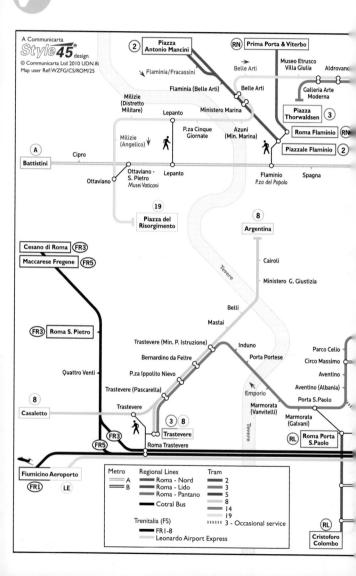

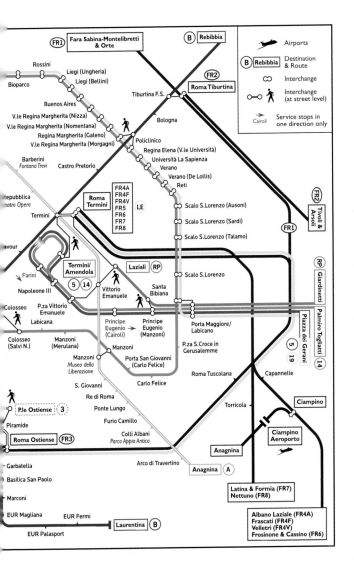

GETTING AROUND

The best way to get around the city centre and ancient sites is by walking. Use public transport for longer trips to the Galleria Borghese, the Vatican Museums and Trastevere, the neighbourhoods of Testaccio, EUR, the catacombs, the excavations at Ostia and Tivoli, or to nearby beaches.

ATAC runs the city's bus, tram and metro system (❶ 06 57003 Ⓦ www.atac.roma.it). Electric minibuses negotiate the narrow backstreets of the old centre. After midnight night buses access most parts of the city until 05.30. Night buses can be identified by an 'N' before the number and an owl symbol above the *bus notturno* timetable. Tickets can be purchased on board.

The bus and tram system is efficient and easy to use, and runs at 05.30–24.00 daily. It also prevents having to deal with Rome's notorious traffic. You can buy a transport map at any tourist information booth or *edicola* (newspaper kiosk).

You can buy a flat-fare ticket for €1. This ticket is valid for as many bus, metro and tram rides as you want within 75 minutes of validation of the ticket. ❶ You need to punch your ticket on all buses and trams (there are yellow ticket-punching machines on each bus and tram).

Tickets are available at the ATAC office, newsstands, tobacconists, and at ticket machines located in all metro stations and at major bus stops. One-, three- and seven-day passes are available for €4, €11 and €16 respectively and allow unlimited public transport travel in the city until midnight of the day of expiry. ❶ There are hefty fines, between €50 and €100, for dodging fares.

If you are planning to travel outside Rome, the BIRG regional transport passes for COTRAL and ATAC services, available in the metro, and at tobacconists and newsstands, are good value. Prices depend on which type of pass you buy. Discounts apply to children under 10, students, disabled people and senior citizens over 70.

Rome's metro (🆆 www.atac.roma.it) runs at 05.30–23.30 on Monday to Thursday and until 01.30 on Friday and Saturday, but in terms of sightseeing it's not that useful. There are only two lines – A (orange) and B (blue) – which are really designed for transporting working commuters in and out of the city. A new C line is under construction, but its first section does not open until 2013. Termini is the hub for these lines, and there are stations at the Colosseum, Piazza Barberini and Piazza di Spagna.

⬤ *The electric minibus No 116 is a convenient way to reach the Villa Borghese*

Taxis can be radio-paged by calling ☎ 06 3570 ☎ 06 4994 or ☎ 06 6645. Be aware that you will have to pay for the driver's time to reach you as well as for the journey itself.

Only yellow or white taxis are fully licensed and equipped with a card, in English, showing the rates and extra charges for luggage, any journeys between 22.00 and 07.00, Sundays and holidays. There are fixed rates for journeys to and from the airport (see page 47). Prices start at €2.80 from Monday to Saturday (€4 on Sunday and holidays), with an additional charge of €0.92 per km.

CAR HIRE

No tourist should even consider driving in Rome proper – parking is limited and non-residents are not allowed to drive in the city centre in an attempt to curb the traffic. However, you can rent a car to explore the countryside. Ask your air carrier if it offers a fly/drive package. All of the following have agencies at Fiumicino and Ciampino Airports, and Termini Rail Station.

Auto Europa ☎ 800 334440 ⓦ www.autoeuropa.it
Avis ☎ 199 100133 ⓦ www.avisautonoleggio.it
Hertz ☎ 199 112211 ⓦ www.hertz.it
Maggiore ☎ 848 867067 ⓦ www.maggiore.it

● *The Fori Imperiali – an ongoing excavation site*

THE CITY OF
Rome

Ancient Rome

For many visitors to Rome the most fascinating and exciting aspect is the chance to see the remains of one of the greatest civilisations ever known. Although nothing remains intact, there are a staggering number of ruins that allow the imagination to re-create a sense of life in times gone by.

This part of Rome encompasses areas that have been especially significant to the city's history. Capitoline Hill was the political hub of the empire, the Washington, DC of its day, whereas the Palatine is also where Rome was founded (according to legend). Mussolini's contributions to Rome and Italy in general are not usually considered successful, but the creation of the Via dei Fori Imperiali is the exception to the rule. It allowed the most concentrated area of ruins around the Forum to become a virtually pedestrianised 'park', leading from one historic gem to another.

SIGHTS & ATTRACTIONS

Il Campidoglio (Capitoline Hill)

One of Rome's seven famous hills, Il Campidoglio was the focal point of imperial politics and still exerts an influence through its gift of the words 'capital' and 'capitol'. The hill was also once home to the Temple of Juno Moneta, over which was built the first Roman mint, giving the world the word 'money'. Today a church, the Santa Maria in Aracoeli, stands on the site.

The focal point of the area today is the Piazza del Campidoglio, originally designed by Michelangelo in 1530 under the auspices of Pope Paul III.

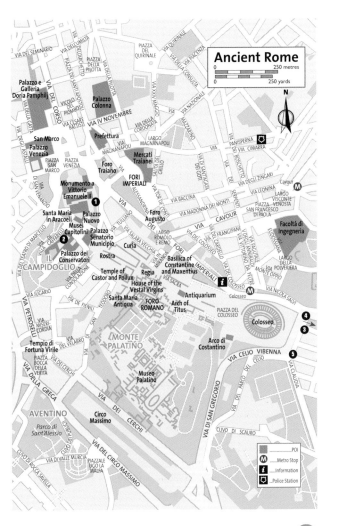

Ancient Rome

0   250 metres

0   250 yards

N

VIA DEL SEMINARIO

VIA DELL'UMILTÀ

VIA DEI LUCCHESI

PIAZZA DEL QUIRINALE

PIAZZA DELLA PILOTTA

VICOLO DEL PIOMBO

VIA DI SANT'EUSTACHIO

VIA DEL CORSO

VIA DELLA PILOTTA

PIAZZA DELLA PILOTTA

VIA DELLA CONSULTA

VIA XXIV MAGGIO

VIA DELLA PIACENZA

Palazzo e Galleria Doria Pamphilj

Palazzo Colonna

VIA CESARE BATTISTI

VIA IV NOVEMBRE

VIA NAZIONALE

San Marco

Prefettura

VIA DELLA CORDONATA

LARGO MAGNANAPOLI

VIA MAGNANAPOLI

VIA PANISPERNA

VIA DI VIA CIMARRA

Palazzo Venezia

PIAZZA SAN MARCO

PIAZZA VENEZIA

Mercati Traianei

MAZZANINO

VIA DI S. AGATA DEI GOTI

VIA DE' BOSCHETTO

VIA DEGLI ZINGARI

Foro Traiano

FORI IMPERIALI

VIA LEONINA

Cavour M

Monumento a Vittorio Emanuele II ❶

VIA ALESSANDRINA

Foro Augusto

VIA MADONNA DEI MONTI

VIA CAVOUR

LARGO VISCONTE VENOSTA

PIAZZA SAN FRANCESCO DI PAOLA

Santa Maria in Aracoeli

Palazzo Nuovo

Musei Capitolini ❷

Palazzo Senatorio

VIA SALARA VECCHIA

VIA TULLIANO

LARGO ROMOLO E REMO

VIA DEL COLOSSEO

VIA DEL FRANGIPANE

Facoltà di ingegneria

EUDOSSIANA

Municipio

Curia

FORI IMPERIALI

VIA ANNIBALDI

VIA DELLE TERME DI TITO

LARGO DELLA POLVERIERA

IL CAMPIDOGLIO

Palazzo dei Conservatori

Rostra

Temple of Castor and Pollux

Regia

Basilica of Constantine and Maxentius

VIA SACRA

MONTE OPPIO

VIA DELLA CONSOLAZIONE

House of the Vestal Virgins

VIA DI MIRANDA

i

VIA NICOLA SALVI

VIA JUGARIO

Santa Maria Antiqua

FORO ROMANO

Antiquarium

Colosseo M

Colosseo

VIA PETROSELLI

VIA DE' FIENILI

Arch of Titus

PIAZZA DEL COLOSSEO

❹

❸

VIA DELLA MISERICORDIA

VIA DEL VELABRO

MONTE PALATINO

VIA SAN TEODORO

Arco di Costantino

VIA CELIO VIBENNA

❺

Tempio di Fortuna Virile

PIAZZA BOCCA DELLA VERITÀ

VIA DEI CERCHI

VIA DI CELIO

VIA CLAUDIA

VIA DELLA GRECA

Museo Palatino

VIA DI SAN GREGORIO

AVENTINO

Parco di Sant'Alessio

Circo Massimo

VIA DEI CERCHI

CLIVO DI SCAURO

CLIVO DI ROCCA SAVELLA

VIA DI VALLE MURCIA

PIAZZALE UGO LA MALFA

VIA DEL CIRCO MASSIMO

POI

M Metro Stop

i Information

Police Station

Nowadays Capitoline Hill is linked to the rest of the city by walkways connecting to the Vittoriano in one direction and to the Roman Forum in the other.

Colosseo (Colosseum)

The Colosseum was built during the heyday of the Roman Empire between AD 70 and 80. Originally, the entire structure was lined with travertine, a local limestone, but over the centuries this was plundered for use elsewhere. It was the largest amphitheatre in Rome (it could hold 55,000 spectators), set in the centre of the city, and it hosted gladiatorial shows, animal hunts and other entertainment. A symbol of great Roman architecture, the construction, though partially in ruins, is still an awesome landmark. ☏ 06 39967700 🌐 www.the-colosseum.net 🕐 daily 09.00–1 hour before sunset 🚌 Bus: 60, 75, 85, 87, 117, 175, 186, 271, 571, 810; Metro: Colosseo ❶ Admission charge (the entrance ticket also gives entry to the Roman Forum and Palatine and is valid for two days – if you plan to see both, buy your ticket at the Palatine to avoid queues!)

Fori Imperiali (Imperial Fora)

Rome is possibly the largest ongoing excavation site in the world, and digs are still under way and uncovering remarkable finds. Since the 1990s a lot of this work has concentrated on the Imperial Fora area around what is now the Via dei Fori Imperiali. The Forum of Trajan (which houses the new Imperial Fora Museum, see page 62) and the Forum of Augustus on the north side are the most interesting. The fora of Vespasian, Nerva and Caesar are also worth a stop. A visitor centre opposite offers guided tours and brochures. There is a new exhibition centre dedicated to the Fora at Via dei Fori

◗ *The Colosseum was the largest amphitheatre in the Roman Empire*

Imperiali on the corner with Via Tempio della Pace (opposite the church of Santi Cosma e Damiano).

Foro Augusto (Forum of Augustus) Just to the east of the Via dei Fori Imperiali is a round brick façade that houses the Order of Malta but was once part of the Forum of Augustus. The original staircase and platform can still be seen of what Augustus dedicated as the Temple of Mars, honouring the god of war after Augustus had successfully avenged his great-uncle's assassins, Brutus and Cassius.

Foro Traiano – Museo dei Fori Imperiali (Forum of Trajan – Museum of the Imperial Fora) One of the most important areas of the Imperial Fora was the Forum of Trajan, a vast area dating from AD 107 that included shops, homes, churches and libraries. It still contains the remarkably well-preserved Mercati di Traiano (Trajan's Markets), which reopened in 2007 after a two-year renovation and now contains a majestic museum. Unearthed from Rome's hills during the Mussolini era (1920s–1930s), the 'Market' was built by Emperor Trajan, best known for conquering the territory that is now Romania, in the 2nd century AD, and is thought of as one of the world's oldest shopping malls (though it was in actual fact probably only partially given over to commercial activities). It is spread over three levels of a series of semicircular halls, and contains what were thought to be 150-odd shops, apartments and offices. Highlights include the main vaulted hall (the Grande Aula) where corn was distributed to the poor, and you can still see the remains of a library. The products of the empire's trade were sold in the market: silks, wine, oil, fruit, flowers and fish.

Outside the museum, visitors can walk around Trajan's Forum, which includes his famous and magnificent 40-m (131-ft) high column, a tribute to the emperor's victory in the wars against Dacia (modern-day Romania) that features carved reliefs documenting his achievements in exacting detail. The bronze statue on top of the column is of St Peter, placed here by Pope Sixtus V in the 16th century. Here you will also find the Via Biberatica (*bibere* is Latin for 'to drink'), which runs between the two sides of the market complex and was probably lined with drinking taverns. (The museum also hosts temporary art shows.) ❸ Via dei Fori Imperiali (The Imperial Fora can only be viewed from the street, apart from Trajan's Forum) ❶ Free admission. Trajan's Forum and Market ❸ Via IV Novembre 94 ❶ 06 0608 ⓦ www.mercatiditraiano.it ⓛ 09.00–19.00 Tues–Sun; last entry 18.00, closed Mon ❿ Bus: 40, 60, 64, 70, 87, 117, 170, 571 ❶ Admission charge

Via dei Fori Imperiali The area now occupied by Via dei Fori Imperiali was once an atmospheric area of Roman and medieval alleyways starting from Piazza Venezia, until Mussolini decided to raze them in 1932 and replace them with this straight, broad street. While much of the original charm of the area may be gone (and with it, undoubtedly, some historic treasures), the street does now make all the ancient sights accessible in a more orderly fashion. The best time to visit is on Sundays, when the road is barred to traffic.

Foro Romano (Roman Forum)

Just to the west of the Via dei Fori Imperiali lies arguably the city's most significant ancient sight, the Roman Forum. This was the heart and soul of the Roman Republic – a place of trade, worship, social gatherings, and political demonstrations and announcements. Even when the increasing population and importance of the city at the advent of the imperial age required further fora, the Roman Forum remained of great importance to the daily life of the citizens.

⬤ The Forum was the bustling heart of the Roman Republic

One of Rome's consuls and rulers, Julius Caesar, realised the need for expansion, and constructed a new senate as well as temples and shops around 50 BC. The work was continued after Caesar's death by his great-nephew and successor, Augustus, and later by the Flavian emperors Vespasian, Nerva and Trajan. Gradually, however, the Forum, much like the empire, began to fall into decay. Many of the buildings were destroyed by a fire in the 3rd century AD, and within a few decades invaders such as the Visigoths left the city in disarray. Building for the future rather than preserving the past was top of the agenda for centuries, and the Forum was often stripped bare to acquire construction materials for other areas. It wasn't until the 19th century, when the burgeoning interest in archaeology was at its zenith, that the historic significance of the area was appreciated and excavations begun.

At first glance the area today may seem little more than rubble and stumps of stone, but as you gradually immerse yourself in the atmosphere it's hard not to marvel that these 2 hectares (5 acres) were once the heart of the Mediterranean world, and the goings-on that occurred here are still of daily significance in the Western world in terms of language, architecture, law and politics. ⓐ Largo della Salaria Vecchia (Via dei Fori Imperiali) ☎ 06 39967700 🕐 daily (Apr–Sept); 09.00–16.30 (Oct–Mar); last entry 1 hour before closing 🚌 Bus: 60, 75, 85, 87, 117, 175, 186, 271, 571, 810; Metro: Colosseo ⓘ Admission charge (ticket also gives entry to the Colosseum and Palatine and is valid for two days)

Antiquarium & Arch of Titus On the Via Sacra, past the church of Santa Maria Nova, is the Antiquarium, the main museum of the site. Exploration of this museum will really contextualise the archaeological wonders discovered here and illustrate why the

Roman Forum proved to be of such historic significance. Within the collection are statue fragments, capitals, tiles, mosaics and friezes, as well as skeletons and wooden coffins exhumed from an Iron Age necropolis found near the Temple of Antoninus and Faustina.

At the top of Via Sacra, thought to be the oldest road in the city, stands the impressive Arch of Titus, built by the emperor's brother Domitian after Titus' death in AD 81. It commemorates his victories in Judaea in AD 70. The structure has been restored many times, and the reliefs can still be seen depicting Titus riding in a chariot with Nike, Goddess of Victory, being escorted by the senate and the people. The opposite side shows spoils such as a menorah being removed from the Temple of Jerusalem.

Basilica of Constantine & Maxentius Opposite the House of the Vestal Virgins (see page 68) is the Temple of Romulus, son of the Emperor Maxentius, built in AD 309. The temple serves as vestibule for the church of Santi Cosima e Damiano. Of importance here is the wonderful 6th-century apse mosaic showing Christ and the Apostles. Past the temple a walkway leads up to the Basilica of Constantine and Maxentius, named after the two emperors who oversaw its construction in the 4th century AD. Once the largest building in the Forum, it is still impressive for its size and construction. Originally it was a place for holding legal proceedings as well as a stock exchange.

The Curia (Senate House) The imposing pillared building at the western end of the Forum is the Curia, originally built by Julius Caesar but rebuilt in the 3rd century AD under Emperor Diocletian. Its original purpose was as the Republic's Senate House and the

◯ *Roman senators met at the Curia, the Senate House*

scene of important political deliberations. At the fall of the empire it became a church and remained in that guise until its restoration in the 20th century.

For a clearer understanding of how Roman politics had such an influence on political procedures today, venture inside and examine the three wide stairs ascending left and right where some 300 Roman senators would sit on their folding chairs to discuss matters of the day. In the middle of these two staircases there's a speakers' platform with a porphyry statue of a figure wearing a toga. Most spectacular, however, not least for the fact that it has managed to survive the centuries, is the original polychrome floor in bright red, yellow, green and white marble. There are also some surviving marble reliefs depicting Emperor Trajan, most likely commissioned by the emperor himself, given the generous light in which he is portrayed. The Plutei of Trajan shows him getting ready to burn public record books in order to relieve Roman citizens of debts to the state; the relief to the right is equally philanthropic, showing him giving money to a woman to indicate his concern for widows and orphans.

The Lapis Niger is a stone which marks the traditional site of the tomb of Romulus. Its steps lead to a monument that was sacred ground during ancient times. The Column of Phocas, across the travertine pavement from the Curia, also known as the Rostra, was the scene of public speeches. To the right of it, the Arch of Septimius Severus was constructed in the 3rd century by his sons, Caracalla and Geta, to mark their father's victories in the Middle East.

House of the Vestal Virgins Beyond the Temple of Vesta is the House of the Vestal Virgins, a 2nd century AD reconstruction of a building originally built by Nero. Vesta was the Roman goddess of the hearth and home, who achieved a cult following during Roman times. The Vestal Virgins were six women who were selected to oversee the Temple of Vesta and keep her sacred flame alight at all times, but were ordered to remain virginal for their full time in 'office' – 30 years from the age of around 10 to 40. The importance of their chastity cannot be overemphasised – the women were buried alive and the violator murdered if they were known to have reneged on this promise. On retirement, the women were accommodated in palaces and were financially secure until their deaths.

Regia When Italy was ruled by the Etruscans, their method of government was monarchical rather than imperial. The three steps flanking the Via Sacra belonged to the Regia, or house of kings – an ancient grouping of foundations that date from the reign of the second king of Rome, Numa, who ruled from 715 to 673 BC. There was a shrine of Mars here that housed the supposed shield and spears of the god of war, which generals embarking on a campaign would rattle before setting off. If the shields and swords rattled of their own accord, however, it was considered a bad omen, and one that required purification and repentance rites.

Across the road from here is the Temple of Antoninus and Faustina, a 2nd-century AD temple still in a remarkable state of preservation, largely because it has been part of the church of San Lorenzo in Miranda since the 7th century. An inscribed lintel connects the six Corinthian columns across the front, dedicating the temple by order of the senate to the god Antonino and the goddess Faustina, the parents of that great military leader Marcus Aurelius. Above the inscription is the roof architrave, along the sides of which can be seen the original frieze of griffins, candelabras and acanthus scrolls. The façade of the church dates back to 1602.

⬥ The Septimius Severus Arch commemorates this emperor's victories

The pile of rubble that is next to the Regia is sadly all that remains of the magnificence that was thought to be the temple to Julius Caesar. A round stone stump under the roof marks the spot where Caesar was cremated after his murder and around which the temple was built.

The broken columns to the right of the Via Sacra mark the site of the Basilica Aemilia, built in the 2nd century BC as a meeting and trade centre. Nearby is a small marble plaque dedicated to Venus Cloacin, marking the site of a small shrine dedicated to Venus where the Cloaca Maxima canal drained the Forum, which was situated on marshland. The Cloaca Maxima reaches all the way to the Tiber from here and still keeps the area drained.

Rostra To the left of the arch is a low wall, the Rostra, one of the most important places in the entire Forum in ancient times. Citizens, traders, senators and interested bystanders gathered to hear important speeches delivered from this spot – it was here that Mark Antony gave his famous celebratory speech about Caesar, following his assassination.

On the left of the Rostra are the stairs of the Basilica Julia, built by Julius Caesar as a law court in 54 BC after his triumphant return from the Gallic Wars. You cannot mount the stairs, as all that remains of the basilica are a few column bases and one nearly complete column.

Further along is the oldest temple in the Forum, the Temple of Saturn, dating from 497 BC. What remains of it are the results of a series of restorations undertaken between 42 BC and as late as AD 380. The temple housed the Roman treasury and mint, but its main focus was during the Saturnalia celebrations each December – a precursor to modern-day Christmas. To the right of this are the remaining columns of the Temple of Vespasian and Titus, built in AD 80. Behind the Arch of Septimius Severus, a pile of bricks is all that is left of the Temple of Concordia Augusta, dedicated by Tiberius in AD 10.

Santa Maria Antiqua & Temple of Castor & Pollux Santa Maria Antiqua on Vicus Tuscus ('Etruscan Street') was the first public building in the area to be converted for Christian worship. Around the corner on the right, the flattened area topped by three Corinthian columns is the Temple of Castor and Pollux.

Monumento a Vittorio Emanuele II
(Monument to Vittorio Emanuele II)

One of the most famous images of Rome is L'Altare della Patria (Vittorio Emanuele Monument). The Vittoriano, as it is known, is built of dazzling white marble excavated from Brescia, and is a flamboyant monument to the first king of Italy after the Unification of 1870. Begun in 1885, its finishing touches were added in 1911.

On either side of the entrance are figures that represent the two seas that surround the Italian peninsula – the Tyrrhenian on the right and the Adriatic on the left. At the top of the stairs is Italy's

---

THE VIA SACRA

The Via Sacra ('Sacred Way') cuts directly through the Forum from below the Capitoline Hill in the west to the far eastern extent of the site and the Arch of Titus, which exits on to the Colosseum. This was the best-known street of Ancient Rome. Victorious emperors and generals rode in glorious processions to give thanks at the Capitoline's Temple of Jupiter.

Tomb of the Unknown Soldier fanned by an eternal flame. Crowning this is a colossal and majestic statue of King Vittorio Emanuele II on horseback; the king's moustache alone measures 3 m (10 ft) in length. The platform it stands on has a frieze depicting figures representing the capital cities of the Italian Republic, while above it the vast pillared gallery stretches the width of the monument with figures symbolising the regions of Italy. The uppermost terrace at the top – the Terrazza delle Quadrighe – was opened to the public for the first time in 2007. Two glass lifts bring visitors up to the terrace every day of the week (and until 23.30 on Fridays and Saturdays).

⬥ *The Monument to Vittorio Emanuele II is one of Rome's best-loved sights*

Inside, the Museo del Risorgimento (Museum of the Resurgence) documents the more than 20-year struggle to unify the country, including a boot worn by patriot leader Giuseppe Garibaldi when he was shot in the foot in 1862. There are excellent explanations in both English and Italian. ⓐ Piazza Venezia ⓣ 06 6991718 ⓦ www.museodelrisorgimento.mi.it ⓛ Monument: daily 09.30–17.30 (summer); 09.30–16.30 (winter); Museum: daily 09.30–18.30; Lift and café: 09.30–18.30 Mon–Thur, 09.30–19.30 Fri–Sun ⓐ Bus: 30, 40, 44, 46, 62, 63, 64, 70, 81, 85, 87, 95, 117, 170, 175, 492, 628, 780, 810, 850 ⓘ Admission charge

Piazza Venezia

It might be hard to imagine today, as you stand amid tooting car horns and watch the white-gloved policemen try to direct the traffic mayhem, that in the 15th century this busy roundabout was a peaceful and grand area dominated by the Palazzo Venezia and its grounds, built by Pope Paul II (see page 77). The *palazzo* also came to prominence in the 20th century as the place of choice for Mussolini to preach to the masses. On the opposite side of the square is the unmissable Vittoriano, a vast white edifice dedicated to King Vittorio Emanuele II, and often nicknamed 'the wedding cake' and 'the typewriter'.

This busy square is an excellent place to start your exploration of Rome. It is close to the medieval and Renaissance sections of the city and the ruins of the ancient city.

San Marco

Next to Palazzo Venezia, on the southern side of the square, is the church of San Marco, a small basilica, built in AD 336 reportedly on the site of the house where St Mark the Evangelist stayed. The façade is recognisable by the statues of lions, the symbol of St Mark, flanking the main entrance. These are almost the only relics of the original medieval church, as well as the 11th-century bell tower and an impressive mosaic depicting the life of Christ dating from the 9th century.

The church was rebuilt in the 5th century and was again reorganised by Pope Paul II in the 15th century when he built Palazzo Venezia. During this time he added his own coat of arms to decorate the church ceiling. It was given its Baroque look in the mid-18th century.

In the portico is the gravestone of Vanozza Catanei, mistress of Rodrigo Borgia, Pope Alexander VI, and mother of the infamous Cesare and Lucretia Borgia. ⓐ Piazza San Marco 48 ❶ 06 6795205 ⓦ www.sanmarcoevangelista.it 🕘 16.00–19.00 Mon, 08.30–12.30, 16.00–19.00 Tue & Thur–Sun, 08.30–12.30 Wed Ⓝ Bus: 30, 40, 44, 46, 62, 63, 64, 70, 81, 85, 87, 95, 117, 170, 175, 492, 628, 780, 810, 850

CULTURE

Musei Capitolini (Capitoline Museums)

The Capitoline Museums' collection is among the most important in a city already awash with treasures. Housed in two Michelangelo-designed *palazzi*, the Palazzo Nuovo and Palazzo dei Conservatori (connected via an underground tunnel), the collection began life in 1471, making it the oldest public exhibition in the world. These days it is an unmissable array of ancient works and Renaissance gems. Most of the statues and paintings are labelled in English and Italian. Make sure you visit the museum café, which has excellent views. ⓐ Piazza del Campidoglio 1 ❶ 06 0608 ⓦ www.museicapitolini.org 🕘 09.00–20.00 Tues–Sun; last entry 19.00, closed Mon Ⓝ Bus: 40, 44,

● *The Musei Capitolini can't fail to impress*

46, 62, 63, 64, 70, 81, 85, 87, 95, 117, 170, 175, 492, 628, 780, 810, 850
ⓘ Admission charge

Palazzo dei Conservatori On the western side of the square, the Palazzo dei Conservatori, formerly the medieval magistrates' court, is the bigger of the two museums, with its focus on statuary and 16th- and 17th-century artworks. Highlights of the first floor include frescoes such as Pietro da Cortona's *Rape of the Sabines*, one of the original bronze statues of the Lo Spinario collection and a marble bust of Medusa.

The second floor is dominated by Renaissance paintings from the 14th century to the 17th century, of which the best known are Caravaggio's shockingly sensual *St John the Baptist*

(c. 1596), Tintoretto's *Penitent Magdalene* (c. 1598), *Baptism of Christ* (c. 1512) by Titian and *Head of a Boy* by Bolognese artist Ludovico Carracci.

Also on the second floor is an enormous picture by Guercino, *The Burial of Santa Petronilla* (1621–3), depicting an early Roman martyr who purportedly was the daughter of St Peter, originally commissioned to hang in St Peter's Basilica.

Palazzo Nuovo Dominating the eastern flank of the Piazza del Campidoglio, the Palazzo Nuovo is accessible from the Palazzo dei Conservatori via the ancient Tabularium (city archive) filled with more sculpture and the remains of a Roman temple.

And sculpture really is the order of the day in this smaller of the two museums. Highlights of the ground floor include *Marforio*, a stone depiction of the river god overlooking the courtyard fountain, plus two versions of a bronze statue of Marcus Aurelius – the 2nd-century original and a copy.

Don't miss the Gabinetto della Venere on the first floor, dedicated entirely to the 1st-century BC *Capitolini Venus*, a delicate piece based on Praxiteles' *Venus of Knidos*. Another Praxiteles copy is the marble 2nd-century BC *Resting Satyr*, which is purported to have inspired the Nathaniel Hawthorne novel *The Marble Faun*. Other highlights include the *Mosaic of the Doves* (which once adorned Hadrian's Villa), the Hall of the Philosophers (among which is the marble bust of Homer), and the poignant *Dying Gaul*, based on a 3rd-century BC Greek original.

Museo Nazionale del Palazzo di Venezia

On the western side of Piazza Venezia, but with its main entrance on Via del Plebiscito, is the eponymous 15th-century Palazzo Venezia, one of the first Renaissance buildings to be constructed in Rome. If it looks strangely familiar, it's probably because you've seen wartime images of Mussolini grinding home his political theories to the masses from the balcony here – the Fascist dictator took over the palazzo as his party headquarters. These days its focus is more on culture than chaos as home to an important collection of Renaissance arts and crafts. Not all works are open to public view, but those paintings that can be seen are some of Italy's most important 15th-century works, such as a portrait of two young men by Giorgione, Borgianni's 16th-century *Deposition of Christ* and Algardi's bust of Pope Innocent X. Temporary exhibitions are also held here, their presence announced by a banner hung on the façade. ⓐ Via del Plebiscito 118 ⓣ 06 69994388 ⓛ 08.30–19.00 Tues–Sun, closed Mon ⓝ Bus: 30, 40, 44, 46, 62, 63, 64, 70, 81, 85, 87, 95, 117, 170, 175, 492, 628, 780, 810, 850 ⓘ Admission charge

RETAIL THERAPY

As this area of the city is filled with remains, there is little of note to buy apart from replicas of ancient statuary at various tourist stalls.

TAKING A BREAK

Museums and shopping are all very well but they do have a habit of whipping up a thirst and an appetite, so take time out to relax every so often at the various appealing cafés in the area.

Caffè Aracoeli £ ❶ This pleasant outdoor café is halfway up the terraces of the Vittoriano and affords good views along with a variety of salads, sandwiches, fruit and snacks. ⓐ Piazza Venezia

📞 06 6991718 🕐 09.30–19.30 Mon–Sat, closed Sun Ⓜ Bus: 30, 40, 44, 46, 62, 63, 64, 70, 81, 85, 87, 95, 117, 170, 175, 492, 628, 780, 810, 850

Caffè Capitolino £ ❷ This museum café offers knockout views from the attractive outdoor terrace. 📍 Piazza del Campidoglio 1
📞 06 82059127 🕐 09.00–19.00 Tues–Sun, closed Mon Ⓜ Bus: 30, 40, 44, 46, 62, 63, 64, 70, 81, 85, 87, 95, 117, 170, 175, 492, 628, 780, 810, 850

AFTER DARK

The area southeast of the Colosseum is home to some lovely local spots, and the liveliest gay bar in Rome. Explore Via Capo d'Africa, Via San Giovanni in Laterano and Via dei Santi Quattro Coronati.

Coming Out £–££ ❸ Across the street from the Colosseum, this is the liveliest and friendliest gay bar/restaurant in Rome. Open all day every day, the clientele spills out noisily into the street until the wee hours. 📍 Via San Giovanni in Laterano 8 📞 06 7009871
🌐 www.comingout.it Ⓜ Bus: 87, 571; Tram: 3; Metro: Colosseo

Luzzi £–££ ❹ A popular neighbourhood eatery just steps from the Colosseum serving tasty pizzas and authentic Roman cuisine. 📍 Via Celimontana 1 📞 06 7096332 🕐 12.00–15.00, 19.30–23.30 Thur–Tues, closed Wed Ⓜ Bus: 87, 571; Tram: 3; Metro: Colosseo

Crab £££ ❺ An upmarket and excellent fish and seafood eatery in a converted warehouse. 📍 Via Capo d'Africa 2 📞 06 77203636
🕐 13.00–15.30, 20.00–23.30 Tues–Sat, 20.00–23.30 Mon (Sept–July), closed Sun Ⓜ Bus: 87, 571; Tram: 3; Metro: Colosseo

Centro storico (historic centre)

In a city that is so intrinsically linked to history at almost every corner, it seems absurd to pinpoint one area as the 'historic centre'. Nevertheless, *centro storico* is the term that is applied to the triangular region around Piazza Navona and surrounded by Rome's main streets (Corso Vittorio Emanuele II and Via del Corso) and the River Tiber. It's a wonderful area in which to spend a day strolling its many alleyways and admiring some of the city's best examples of classical and Baroque architecture. The following sights and attractions are presented in the order we suggest you visit them for maximum enjoyment.

SIGHTS & ATTRACTIONS

Campo de' Fiori

In the rough-and-tumble world of the Middle Ages, right through to the Renaissance, the Campo de' Fiori (literally 'Field of Flowers') was a hive of activity due to its daily market. But it was also a place of intrigue, murder and execution. Among those who met their fate here was the 16th-century philosopher Giordano Bruno, who stood firm against the Inquisition and was burnt at the stake in return. Today a statue of the martyr is the focal point of the square.

Following long-standing tradition, there is still a bustling market here every morning, offering a wonderful array of colours from the numerous fruit and vegetable stalls. It's a fascinating place to enjoy an outdoor drink at one of the many cafés on the square and soak up the atmosphere. ⓐ Campo de' Fiori ⓛ Market 07.00–13.30 Mon–Sat, closed Sun ⓝ Bus: 30, 40, 62, 64, 70, 81, 87, 116, 492, 571, 628

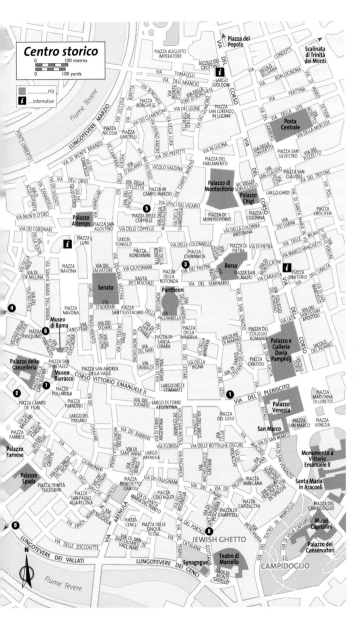

Jewish Ghetto

Situated to the east of Via Arenula is the area historically known as
the Jewish Ghetto. Rome's Jewish population dates back to the 2nd
century BC, and for centuries they were integrated into society with
little or no prejudice. All this was to change, however, during the
period of the Inquisition and the Counter-Reformation, and between
1555 and 1559 Pope Paul VI ordered that the entire Jewish
community must live within a walled and decidedly unpleasant
enclosure. From then on, right up until the Unification of Italy, and
as a chilling precursor to what would happen in the 20th century,
any Jew venturing out of the ghetto was required to wear a yellow
cap and shawl as a means of religious identification.

Today the former ghetto is home to Rome's largest **synagogue**;
its museum offers a fascinating insight into the history of the
building and the Jewish community of the city (ⓐ Lungotevere dei
Cenci ❶ 06 68400661 Ⓦ www.museoebraico.roma.it Ⓛ 10.00–18.15
Sun–Thur, 10.00–15.15 Fri (mid-June–mid-Sept); 10.00–16.15
Sun–Thur, 09.00–13.15 Fri (mid-Sept–mid-June); closed Jewish
holidays). Entry is by guided tour (in English) only – the synagogue
was attacked by the Palestine Liberation Organisation (PLO) in 1982,
and has been under police guard ever since.

Palazzo Altemps

Another important Roman family, the Altemps, bought this 15th-
century palazzo in 1568 and, again, used it to house and expand their
impressive art collection. In 1997, following a painstaking restoration,
the building was incorporated into the Museo Nazionale Romano as
a home for a breathtaking collection of classical sculpture.

Much of the collection was acquired in the 17th century by
Cardinal Ludovico Ludovisi. Among the masterpieces are a bust of

⬢ *The Portico d'Ottavia in the Jewish Ghetto*

the philosopher Demosthenes from the 2nd century AD, a statue entitled *Athena with Serpent* and a Roman copy of a Greek *Galata's Suicide*, which is thought to have been commissioned by Julius Caesar. There is also a statue of Ares that was repaired by Bernini in 1621, and several erotic works, the delightful *Pan and Daphne*, a *Satyr and Nymph*, and the muses Calliope and Urania. Additionally, there's a 5th-century BC 'throne' with carved reliefs. ⓐ Via di Sant'Apollinare 46 ⓣ 06 39967700 ⓛ 09.00–19.45 Tues–Sun, closed Mon ⓝ Bus: 30, 70, 81, 87, 116, 130, 186, 492, 628 ⓘ Admission charge (the entrance ticket allows entry into all four Museo Nazionale Romano sites and is valid for three days)

Palazzo Farnese

This is one of the gems of the Renaissance period (the second act of Giacomo Puccini's 1900 opera *Tosca* is set here). The palace was begun for Cardinal Alessandro Farnese (later Pope Paul III, 1534–49) by Antonio da Sangallo the Younger in 1514. After da Sangallo's death in 1546, Michelangelo took over, adding the upper storey and cornice. He planned a riverside wing and bridge, but only a single arch of the bridge was built over the Via Giulia, linking the palace with the Villa Farnesina (see page 114) in Trastevere. Inside, on the first floor are ceiling frescoes by the Carracci brothers, Agostino and Annibale (1597–1603), depicting scenes from Ovid's *Metamorphoses*. Palazzo Farnese now houses the French Embassy. ⓐ Piazza Farnese ⓣ 06 68892818 ⓦ www.france-italia.it ⓛ 50-minute tours in Italian and French are held at 15.00, 16.00, 17.00 on Mon and Thur (Sept–late July); book 1 to 4 months in advance by email ⓔ visitefarnese@france-italia.it (or download form online). Bring photo ID
ⓝ Bus: 40, 46, 62, 64, 70, 81, 87, 116, 280, 492, 571, 628, 916

Pantheon

Looming down over Piazza della Rotunda, the Pantheon, along with the Colosseum, stands today as the most complete Ancient Roman structure in the city. There has been a temple here since 27 BC during Marcus Agrippa's rule, but it was entirely rebuilt by Emperor Hadrian in the early 2nd century AD.

One of Hadrian's most remarkable additions was the domed roof at a staggering size of 43 m by 43 m (142 ft by 142 ft). At one time the entire roof was also cast in bronze, but this was melted down in the 17th century under the orders of Pope Urban VIII in order to make the *baldacchino* (canopy) for St Peter's Basilica in the Vatican. The Pantheon was consecrated as a church in the 7th century after the discovery of Christian bones on the site.

🔺 *The Pantheon – an almost complete Ancient Roman structure*

Since the 19th century the Pantheon has also been used as the burial place of Italian monarchs, including the first king of Italy, Vittorio Emanuele II. The artist Raphael is also buried here. ⓐ Piazza della Rotonda ⓞ 06 68300230 ⓛ 08.30–19.30 Mon–Sat, 09.00–18.00 Sun ⓝ Bus: 40, 46, 62, 70, 87, 116, 492, 628, 810

Piazza Navona

If anywhere can be described as the heart of this rambling city, it must surely be Piazza Navona, and no visit is complete without soaking up the atmosphere of this beautiful square. The area was originally used for chariot races but the majority of its current appearance dates from the 17th century when beautiful *palazzi* and churches were commissioned by Pope Innocent X. Among the first was the church of Sant'Agnese in Agone, designed by Borromini and supposedly built on the site where the 13-year-old St Agnes was stripped naked in front of the entire city in the 3rd century AD for her religious views.

The full length of the square is punctuated by three Baroque fountains, all designed by Bernini around 1651. The central Fontana dei Quattro Fiumi (Fountain of the Four Rivers) is the most famous, with each figure representing the most important rivers in that period: the Nile, the Danube, the Ganges and the Plate. The Fontana del Moro (Fountain of the Moor) at the southern end of the square depicts, as its name suggests, the figure of a North African Moor, while the Fontana del Nettuno (Neptune's Fountain) shows the sea god wrestling with a sea monster.

Bustling day and night, the pedestrianised square is one of the most popular places in Rome to enjoy a coffee, an aperitif or a full meal, as well as an animated gossip, at one of the numerous cafés whose tables spill on to the pavement in summer. ⓝ Bus: 70, 81, 87

CULTURE

Museo Barracco

If you're into ancient sculpture, don't miss the small but impressive collection at the Museo Barracco. There is a range of pieces from Ancient Greece and Egypt including sphinxes, friezes and ceramics. ⓐ Corso Vittorio Emanuele II 166a ⓣ 06 68806848 ⓦ www.museobarracco.it ⓛ 09.00–19.00 Tues–Sun, closed Mon ⓝ Bus: 40, 46, 62, 64, 116, 492, 571, 916 ⓘ Admission charge

Galleria Doria Pamphilj

One of Rome's most important families, the Doria Pamphiljs, has been in ownership of this 15th-century *palazzo* since 1647. Today the

⬤ The Fontana dei Quattro Fiumi with Sant'Agnese in the background

family's spectacular art collection is open to public view, and includes works by masters from all over Europe. Highlights include portraits of Pope Innocent X by Bernini and Velázquez, Dutch and Flemish artworks including Hans Memling's *Deposition*, two paintings by Caravaggio (*Mary Magdalene* and *John the Baptist*) and Titian's *Salome with the Head of St John*. Furnishings include Venetian chandeliers and Belgian tapestries. ⓐ Piazza del Collegio Romano (entrance at Via del Corso 305) ⓣ 06 6797323 ⓦ www.doriapamphilj.it ⓛ daily 10.00–17.00 ⓝ Bus: 62, 63, 81, 85, 117, 119, 160, 175, 492, 628, 850 ⓘ Admission charge

Museo di Roma (Museum of Rome)

The Museo di Roma is in the Palazzo Braschi, built at the end of the 18th century. In 1952 the palace became a museum dedicated to the history of Rome since the Middle Ages. Its collection of sculpture, clothing, furniture, photography and old books examines the city from the Middle Ages to the early 20th century. There are busts and portraits of popes and cardinals, fragments of frescoes and mosaics from the old basilica of St Peter's, and views of the city through the ages. ⓐ Via di San Pantaleo 10 ⓣ 06 0608 ⓦ www.museodiroma.it ⓛ 09.00–19.00 Tues–Sun, closed Mon ⓝ Bus: 30, 40, 46, 62, 64, 81, 87, 116, 190, 492, 571, 628, 916 ⓘ Admission charge

RETAIL THERAPY

Diego Percossi Papi For a stunning necklace, bracelet or any other jewellery visit this shop specialising in Renaissance designs. ⓐ Piazza Sant'Eustachio 16 ⓣ 06 68801466 ⓦ www.percossipapi.com ⓛ 16.00–19.30 Mon, 10.00–13.00, 16.00–19.30 Tues–Sat, closed Sun ⓝ Bus: 40, 46, 62, 70, 87, 116, 492, 628, 810

Spazio Sette Located in a former cardinal's palace featuring original frescoed ceilings, Spazio Sette sells furniture, housewares and other goods by the best names in international and Italian design. ❸ Via dei Barbieri 7 ❶ 06 6869747 ❺ 15.30–19.30 Mon, 09.30–13.00, 15.30–19.30 Tues–Sat, closed Sun ❻ Bus: 30, 40, 46, 62, 64, 70, 81, 87, 116, 628, 916

TAKING A BREAK

Enoteca Corsi £ ❶ A gem of a find between Piazza Venezia and the Pantheon. A highly traditional Roman trattoria and wine shop that serves a limited but delicious menu of whatever the owners happen to have cooked that morning. Very busy at lunchtime, but worth the wait. ❸ Via del Gesù 87 ❶ 06 6790821 ❺ Mon–Sat lunch, closed Sun ❻ Bus: 23, 30, 46, 62, 63, 64, 70, 81, 87, 492, 628, 630, 780, 916; Tram: 8

Il Forno di Campo de' Fiori £ ❷ Great place for classic pizzas such as *pizza bianca* (drizzled with olive oil) and *pizza rossa* (with a tiny smear of tomato sauce) piping hot from the wood-fired oven. Has a deservedly loyal clientele. ❸ Campo de' Fiori 22 ❶ 06 68806662 ❺ 07.30–14.30, 16.45–20.00 Mon–Fri, 07.30–14.30 Sat (July & Aug); 07.30–14.30, 16.45–20.00 Mon–Sat (Sept–June); closed Sun ❻ Bus: 30, 40, 46, 62, 64, 70, 81, 87, 116, 186, 204, 492, 628, 916

La Tazza d'Oro £ ❸ Come here for the smoothest, richest cappuccino in town. Their Miscela Regina blend is roasted on-site five times a week and you can buy it to take home, too. In summer replace your coffee with their famed *granita al caffè* (sweet espresso poured over crushed ice). ❸ Via degli Orfani 84 ❶ 06 6789792 ❼ www.tazzadorocoffeeshop.com ❺ 07.00–20.00 Mon–Sat, closed Sun ❻ Bus: 30, 40, 64, 70, 87, 116

AFTER DARK

Da Baffetto £–££ ❹ A tiny neighbourhood favourite, famous for its enormous pizzas (you may want to share one between two), as well as for its bruschetta with toppings such as white beans and fresh vegetables. Good value, with tables outside in summer, but do be prepared to queue, especially in the evening. ⓐ Via del Governo Vecchio 114, off Piazza Pasquino ❶ 06 6861617 ⓛ daily 19.00–24.00 ⓝ Bus: 30, 40, 46, 62, 64, 70, 81, 116, 492, 628

Caffè Riccioli ££ ❺ This Japanese restaurant boasts stylish dining rooms and platters of excellent sashimi, along with beef and seafood dishes and delicious desserts. ⓐ Piazza delle Coppelle 13 ❶ 06 68210313 ⓦ www.ricciolicafe.com ⓛ 09.00–01.00 Mon–Sat, closed Sun ⓝ Bus: 64, 70, 87, 116, 186

Cul de Sac ££ ❻ The oldest wine bar in town with an enviable collection of wines (many to be consumed by the glass) and an interesting menu of one-off dishes, salads and mouthwatering plates of cold meats and cheeses from all over Italy. ⓐ Piazza Pasquino 73 ❶ 06 68801094 ⓛ 24 hrs ⓝ Bus: 30, 40, 64, 70, 81, 87, 116, 186, 492, 628

Ditirambo ££ ❼ A buzzy restaurant where the pasta, bread and sweets are all made in-house. The menu is varied and will satisfy all palates. ⓐ Piazza della Cancelleria 74 ❶ 06 6871626 ⓦ www.ristoranteditirambo.it ⓛ 19.30–23,30 Mon, 13.00–15.00, 19.30–23.30 Tues–Sun ⓝ Bus: 40, 62, 64, 116, 916

Giggetto al Portico D'Ottavia ££ ❽ In existence since 1923, three generations of the Ceccarelli family have owned this establishment.

It's the only place in Rome where you can get traditional Italian kosher food: try the *carciofi alla Giudea* (Jerusalem artichokes made the Jewish way) or the *baccalà* (salt cod). ⓐ Via del Portico d'Ottavia 21a–22 ⓣ 06 6861105 ⓦ www.giggettoalporticodottavia.it ⓝ Bus: 23, 40, 64, 70, 271, 630, 780

Glass Hostaria £££ ❾ Cross the Ponte Sisto to Trastevere for excellent taster menus and creative dishes and desserts in an inviting minimalist setting. This is a memorable gourmet dining experience. ⓐ Vicolo del Cinque 58 ⓣ 06 58335903 ⓦ www.glass-hostaria.com ⓛ 20.00–23.30 Tues–Sun, closed Mon ⓝ Bus: H; Tram: 8

🔺 *Rome's piazze are great for alfresco dining*

Via del Corso & Tridente

Via del Corso borders the historic centre on its eastern side, stretching from Piazza Venezia in the south to Piazza del Popolo in the north. A walk along this major artery offers various turn-offs to admire lovely *palazzi*, churches and squares. Shopaholics should not miss the opportunity to explore the many stylish clothing and accessories stores in the roads between Piazza del Popolo and Piazza di Spagna.

SIGHTS & ATTRACTIONS

Scalinata di Trinità dei Monti (Spanish Steps)

These beautiful broad, tiered steps and the adjoining Piazza di Spagna get their name from the Spanish Embassy that used to have

▲ *The Scalinata di Trinità dei Monti (Spanish Steps) are a popular meeting place*

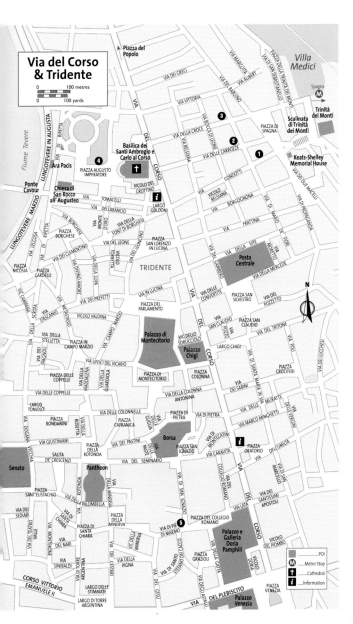

its headquarters here. The steps were constructed in 1725 by Francisco de Sanctis as a means of reaching the Trinità dei Monti church at the top of the hill, and the three tiers were intended to reflect the three figures of the Holy Trinity.

Their popularity as a general meeting place and social spot began in the 18th century at the height of the Grand Tour period as most hotels and boarding houses were located in that area.
ⓐ Trinità dei Monti Ⓝ Metro: Spagna

Via del Corso

Over the years, Via del Corso has been home to numerous notable expats: the German poet Goethe once lived at No 18, while the Romantic poet Percy Bysshe Shelley and his wife Mary resided in No 375 (now a bank).

Just off Via del Corso, about halfway along, is Piazza Colonna, named after the impressive 1st-century AD column commemorating the military successes of Marcus Aurelius with a variety of carved reliefs. The square also contains the official residence of the prime minister.

CULTURE

Ara Pacis

Augustus' Altar of Peace was commissioned by the senate in 13 BC to celebrate the Augustan peace and inaugurated in 9 BC. The original altar was located in the Campo Marzio area not far away but was probably destroyed during the Barbarian invasions in the 5th and 6th centuries AD. Early in the 1900s pieces of it were found in excavations and museums in Italy and France. In the 1930s its reconstruction was ordered by Mussolini. It was relocated to its current address and

housed in a pavilion designed by Vittorio Morpurgo in 1938. The pavilion was recently replaced by a 1,500 sq m (16,000 sq ft) new museum complex designed by American architect Richard Meier.
🅐 Lungotevere in Augusta (north of Via Tomacelli) ☎ 06 0608
🅦 www.arapacis.it 🕒 09.00–19.00 Tues–Sun, closed Mon 🚌 Bus: 81, 117, 119, 224, 590, 628, 913, 926; Metro: Spagna ❶ Admission charge

Keats-Shelley Memorial House
Facing on to the Piazza di Spagna, on the southern side of the foot of the Spanish Steps, is the Keats-Shelley Memorial House. It was set up as a library in honour of the poet John Keats, who died here at the age of 25 in 1821, and Percy Bysshe Shelley, poet and husband of *Frankenstein* author Mary Shelley. Manuscripts and mementos of

🔺 *The reconstructed Ara Pacis is housed inside this modern pavilion*

these and other Romantic poets are on display within the elegant rooms. ⓐ Piazza di Spagna 26 ❶ 06 6784235 ⓦ www.keats-shelley-house.org ⓛ 09.00–13.00, 15.00–18.00 Mon–Fri, 11.00–14.00, 15.00–18.00 Sat; guided tours by appointment; closed Sun Ⓝ Metro: Spagna ❶ Admission charge

Piazza del Popolo

The Piazza del Popolo evolved over many centuries. The triple-arched Porta del Popolo, the church of Santa Maria del Popolo (designed and adorned by Bramante, Bernini and Raphael, among other heady Renaissance talents), the Pincio gardens, and the twin churches of Santa Maria di Monte Santo (1672–5, by Bernini, Carlo Fontana and Carlo Rainaldi) and Santa Maria dei Miracoli (Carlo Rainaldi, 1675–9) all border the piazza. In the square's centre is an obelisk from the Circus Maximus, brought to Rome in 10 BC. The lions at its base are 19th century. This (thankfully) now almost entirely traffic-free square is one of the most beautiful *piazze* in Italy. ⓐ Piazza del Popolo Ⓝ Bus: 81, 95, 117, 119, 224, 590, 628, 913, 926; Tram: 2; Metro: Flaminio

RETAIL THERAPY

Via Condotti, just south of Piazza di Spagna, is one of the best-known shopping streets in Rome and is definitely the place to come if you're after the big names in Italian and designer fashion, jewellery and leather goods.

Bulgari If you're not among the lucky few who can afford these jewellery prices, the window designs are worth seeing. ⓐ Via Condotti 10 ❶ 06 696261 ⓛ 15.30–19.30 Mon, 10.30–19.30 Tues–Sat, closed Sun Ⓝ Metro: Spagna

Campanile One of the best places for high-quality, if expensive, leather goods such as handbags and belts. 🏠 Via Condotti 58 📞 06 6783041 🕐 15.30–19.30 Mon, 10.30–19.30 Tues–Sat, closed Sun 🚇 Metro: Spagna

Energie One of Rome's most popular stores, aimed primarily at teenagers and 20-somethings with expensive and trendy tastes in fashion (part of the Miss Sixty group). 🏠 Via del Corso 179 📞 06 6781045 🕐 daily 10.00–20.00 🚌 Bus: 30, 40, 44, 46, 62, 63, 64, 70, 81, 85, 87, 95, 117, 170, 175, 492, 628, 780, 810, 850

Fendi Rome-born fashion giant Fendi (now owned by the Louis Vuitton group) took over a large 19th-century neoclassical *palazzo* a few years ago and opened a flagship store. Come for its famed leather accessories and Karl Lagerfeld-designed women's lines. 🏠 Largo Goldoni 419 📞 06 696661 🌐 www.fendi.com 🕐 daily 10.30–19.00

Furla Furla makes genuine and well-crafted leather handbags and accessories in contemporary or classic styles, and in eye-popping or more subdued tones. What's more, these delectable treats come at affordable prices. 🏠 Piazza di Spagna 22 📞 06 69200363 🌐 www.furla.it 🕐 10.00–20.00 Mon–Sat, 10.30–20.00 Sun 🚇 Metro: Spagna

TAKING A BREAK

Antico Caffè Greco £ ❶ Follow in the footsteps of Keats, Shelley and Wagner among others, and enjoy a cake and coffee amid Baroque mirrors and plush red velvet seating. (It's a bit of a tourist trap these

days and there's certainly better and cheaper fare elsewhere.)
 Via Condotti 86 06 6791700 10.30–19.00 Sun & Mon,
09.00–19.30 Tues–Sat Metro: Spagna

AFTER DARK

Al 31 ££ ❷ Neighbourhood locale serving meat-centric Umbrian
and classic Roman fare to a throng of regulars and tourists. Outdoor
seating in fine weather, and some fish, too. Via delle Carrozze 31
 06 6786127 www.hostariaal31.com 12.15–15,00, 19.00–22.30
Mon–Sat, closed Sun Bus: 117, 119, 913; Metro: Spagna

Otello alla Concordia ££ ❸ Good, fresh, typically Roman food served by
friendly staff in a mossy, wisteria-filled courtyard in summer and elegant
vaulted dining rooms with starched linens in winter. Via della Croce 81
 06 6791178 www.otelloallaconcordia.it 12.30– 15.00, 19.30–23.00
Mon–Sat, closed Sun Bus: 117, 119, 913; Metro: Spagna

Tatì ££ ❹ The most recently opened arm of the 'Gusto gourmet
empire across the square at No 9 (which includes a pizzeria,
restaurant, wine bar, kitchen supplies store and *osteria*), a marine-
themed cocktail bar and café (downstairs) and fish-and-vegetable
restaurant (upstairs), is a good place for lunch, drinks or dinner.
 Piazza Augusto Imperatore 28 06 68134221 www.gusto.it
 Bus: 81, 117, 119, 224, 590, 628, 913, 926; Metro: Spagna

Green T ££–£££ ❺ A relaxed but upmarket Chinese restaurant that
has really raised the bar for the country's cuisine. Via di Piè di
Marmo 28 06 6798628 www.green-tea.it 12.30–15.00,
19.30–24.00 Mon–Sat, closed Sun Bus: 81, 116, 117, 119, 590, 628

Vatican City & Prati

On the west bank of the Tiber lies the Vatican City State, the smallest independent state in the world, covering just over 40 hectares (100 acres). The state was established as an autonomous sovereignty in 1929 after agreement between the king of Italy and the papacy acknowledged that the Church could not be ruled under political regimes but needed to establish its own rules according to the Roman Catholic faith. Today, the Vatican is populated by fewer than 1,000 citizens and has its own militia, the Swiss Guards.

The area might be small in terms of world geography. However, it can take visitors several days to explore the entire area and only the very dedicated will have the stamina to do so.

The public entrance into Vatican City is through Bernini's glorious Piazza San Pietro (St Peter's Square), which offers a breathtaking introduction to the glories that are to come. Straight in front is the towering façade of St Peter's Basilica and the pillared colonnade decorated with statues of 140 saints. In front of this is an obelisk brought here from the Ancient Egyptian city of Heliopolis and two fountains also placed here by Bernini.

❶ Proper dress is required for visiting the Vatican; this means long trousers or knee-length skirts, covered shoulders (no sleeveless tops) and no bare feet, or you will not be allowed into the Vatican, St Peter's or any of the museums.

CULTURE

Basilica di San Pietro (St Peter's Basilica)
Arguably the best-known and most recognisable church in the Christian world, and the seat of the Catholic Church, St Peter's took

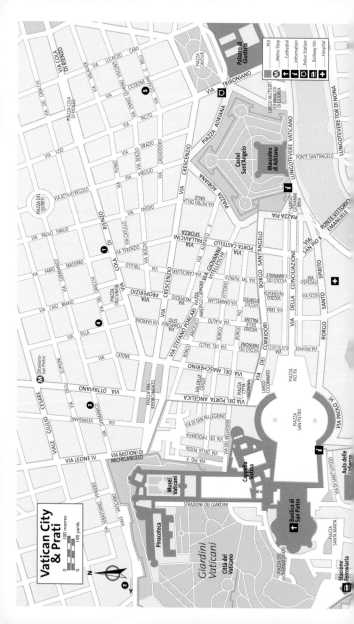

more than 100 years to build, from 1506 to 1626. During that time some of the greatest names of the Renaissance contributed to its glorious whole. It takes its name from the supposed burial site of St Peter, and a church had existed here since the 4th century AD, commissioned by the first Christian emperor, Constantine.

The first architect to lend his services to the new basilica was Bramante, who suggested the Greek Cross design topped by a central dome. After his death in 1514, the responsibility for completing the dome fell to Michelangelo, who worked on the project for nearly 20 years until his own death in 1564. The finished dome, probably the most famous in the world, was completed in 1590 by Giacomo della Porta, entirely to Michelangelo's original designs. The scale of the dome leaves no doubt as to how important this church was to be, at 120 m (394 ft) in height and 42 m (138 ft) in diameter. The sheer beauty of the structure went on to influence the design of many other landmark buildings around the world, among them London's St Paul's Cathedral, Les Invalides in Paris and the Capitol Building in Washington, DC.

Carlo Maderno was the final architect to work on the structure of the church from 1605 onwards, including the pillared façade, and he turned it into a Latin plan that followed Constantine's original church.

❶ Proper dress is required to go inside the church; no shorts or bare shoulders are allowed.

Much of the quite stunning interior owes its Baroque splendour to the sculptor Gian Lorenzo Bernini, who was a real superstar of that genre. A major flourish is the flamboyant baldacchino (canopy) that protects St Peter's tomb.

On the right side of the nave, behind protective glass since a crazed axe attack in 1972, is Michelangelo's beautiful *Pietà*.

MUSEI VATICANI (VATICAN MUSEUMS)

The Vatican Museums are a vast collection of rooms and galleries to the north of St Peter's Basilica, housed in former papal palaces largely dating from the 15th and 16th centuries. The most famous area of the museums, and the one to which all visitors gravitate, is the Sistine Chapel (see page 104), but if you have the time and the stamina there are priceless collections to view in other parts of the complex.

The Pinacoteca is the main art gallery of the museums and features a stunning array of works, including some by Leonardo da Vinci. The Raphael Rooms conserve frescoes that were commissioned from the great artist by Pope Julius II. Other stunning 15th-century frescoes can be seen in the Borgia Apartment.

Classical statuary, largely Roman copies of Greek originals, can be seen in both the Pio-Clementine and Pio-Christian Museums, including the famous Apollo Belvedere.

There are also museums dedicated to finds from Ancient Egypt and from the Etruscan era.

In the middle of the museum complex are three courtyards: the Cortile del Belvedere at the southern end, the small Cortile della Biblioteca in the middle, created by the

Completed when he was just 25, it clearly shows his genius in sculpting the human body. Further on, in the right transept is a sculpture of Pope Clement XIII by Canova, then a 13th-century bronze of St Peter, said to be by Arnolfo di Cambio. Under Michelangelo's dome is the *baldacchino* (c. 1524), a 29-m (96-ft) high canopy made from the bronze stripped from the Pantheon roof.

construction of the Vatican Library and Braccio Nuovo, and the northernmost of the three, Cortile della Pigna, named after the huge bronze *pigna* (pine cone) mounted in the niche at the end. If you are on a guided tour, you will be stopped here to talk through the Sistine Chapel paintings before going in, as it is forbidden to speak inside.

The former main entrance to the museums was created by Pope Pius XI in 1932, and its huge bronze spiral staircase, in a double helix design, the work of Giuseppe Momo, made a fitting monumental prelude to the ticket offices above. On it are displayed the heraldic arms of all the popes from 1447 to 1922 – Nicholas II to Pius XI's predecessor Benedict XV. Sadly, the museum entrance was recently updated and restructured so that you now enter through a door in the bastion wall to the left of Pius XI's entrance, through a large hall and a new marble staircase. An escalator carries you up to the museums. It's not necessary to take a guided tour, although this will give you greater insight into the collections. If you prefer to be independent and selective, remember that you must follow the one-way system and that some collections can be closed or moved around with little notice. Refer to the website (ⓦ www.vatican.va) for up-to-date information.

A visit to the treasury is worthwhile to view a portion of the jewels that make up the riches of the Catholic Church.

Another must-see is the tombs of the ancient and modern popes at the Vatican Grottoes. Behind a wall of glass is the supposed tomb of St Peter. Leaving the grottoes, exit into a courtyard and the ticket office for the climb (or lift) up to Michelangelo's dome. Once you reach the top the views over Rome are stupendous. ⓐ Piazza San Pietro ① 06 69883712 ⓦ www.vatican.va ⓛ Basilica: daily 07.00–19.00 (Apr–Sept); 07.00–18.30 (Oct–Mar); Grottoes: daily 09.00–18.00 (Apr–Sept); 09.00–17.00 (Oct–Mar); Dome: daily 08.00–18.00 (Apr–Sept); 08.00–17.00 (Oct–Mar) ⓝ Bus: 23, 40, 62, 64, 115, 116, 492, 571; Metro: Ottaviano-San Pietro, then a long walk

ⓘ If you want to tour the *necropolis vaticana* (the area around St Peter's tomb), you must apply in advance at the Uficio Scavi through the arch to the left of the stairs up the basilica (① 06 69885318). You leave your name, number in your party and the dates you would like to visit and you will then be notified by telephone with the date, time and price of your tour.

There are 12 museums connected with the Vatican (see page 102), but the absolute unmissable is the **Cappella Sistina** (Sistine Chapel).

⬥ *The stunning St Peter's Basilica at night*

VATICAN PRACTICALITIES

The Vatican Museums and St Peter's Basilica are open to visitors (no shorts or bare shoulders), and it is also possible to visit the Vatican Gardens, though only on one guided tour a day (🕑 09.30 Mon, Tues & Thur–Sat; closed Wed, Sun and religious holidays). It costs around €12, lasts approximately two hours and tickets must be bought from the **Vatican Information Office** in Piazza San Pietro (☎ 06 69882350 🌐 www.vaticanstate.va) or online at 🌐 http://biglietteriamusei.vatican.va. You can attend a papal audience, usually held on Wednesdays at 11.00 in the Audiences Hall, but remember that these are not one-on-one affairs – hundreds of other people will be there, too. It's possible to get a ticket if you apply no more than a month and not less than two days in advance, by sending a fax with your name, home address and your preferred date of audience to the **Prefettura della Casa Pontificia** (☎ 06 69884857 🖷 06 69885863).

Finally, if you want to send a postcard with a Vatican postmark, there are Vatican post offices on the north side of Piazza San Pietro and inside the Vatican Museums.

Pope Julius II commanded the young artistic genius Michelangelo to decorate the ceilings of the pope's Chapel with frescoes, a project that was to take four years of constant labour between 1508 and 1512. Michelangelo despised the project, not only for its difficulty, suspended from scaffolding, but because he was keen to devote his time to sculpture, but the final result was to prove to be arguably his most famous work and one of the finest artworks in the world.

⬥ *The Cappella Sistina (Sistine Chapel) – Michelangelo's masterpiece*

The most famous of some 33 ceiling panels are the *Creation of Adam* and the *Creation of Eve*, but there are many other panels that depict other parts of the Book of Genesis. On the altar wall is the *Last Judgement*, completed 20 years after the frescoes when Michelangelo was in his 60s. Other wall frescoes are by Renaissance painters such as Botticelli, Perugino, Pinturicchio and Ghirlandaio. ⓐ Viale Vaticano ☎ 06 69884676 ⓦ www.vatican.va ⏰ 09.00–18.00 Mon–Sat, last entry 16.00; 09.00–14.00 last Sun of each month, 12.30 last entry ⓝ Tram: 19; Metro: Ottaviano-San Pietro or Cipro ⓘ Admission charge (tickets can be purchased online at ⓦ http://biglietteriamusei.vatican.va)

RETAIL THERAPY

There are a few shops in Vatican City and in the museums. St Peter's Square is crammed with outdoor vendors selling souvenirs.

TAKING A BREAK

Franchi £ ❶ A traditional deli that is also a high-end *tavola calda* serving cooked meals for lunch, such as *pasta e ceci* (pasta and chickpea stew) or sweet-and-sour salt cod. ⓐ Via Cola di Rienzo 200–204 ☎ 06 6874651 ⓦ www.franchi.it ⏰ 08.15–21.00 Mon–Sat, closed Sun

Pizzarium £ ❷ Just opposite the Cipro metro stop, this unremarkable pizzeria sells succulent pizza by the slice and fried Italian street food specialities such as *supplì* and *arancini* (rice balls with different fillings). ⓐ Via della Meloria 43 ☎ 06 39745416 ⓝ Bus: 180, 490, 496, 913; Metro: Cipro

AFTER DARK

Dal Toscano ££ ❸ Famous for its succulent Tuscan T-bone steaks at honest prices and its efficient service. Try its mouthwatering rice fritters for dessert. Book if you can. ⓐ Via Germanico 58–60 ☎ 06 39725717 🌐 www.ristorantedaltoscano.it 🕒 12.30–15.00, 20.00–23.00 Tues–Sun, closed Mon 🚍 Bus: 23, 32, 34, 40, 49, 62, 81, 280, 491, 590; Tram: 19; Metro: Ottaviano-San Pietro

Il Matriciano ££–£££ ❹ An upmarket restaurant – and Prati institution – conveniently located near St Peter's serving regional specialities. There's an inviting pavement terrace. ⓐ Via dei Gracchi 55 ☎ 06 3212327 🕒 12.30–15.00, 20.00–23.30 Sun–Fri (summer); 12.30–15.00, 20.00–23.30 Thur–Tues (winter) 🚇 Metro: Ottaviano-San Pietro

L'Arcangelo £££ ❺ This place just north of Piazza Cavour is a real food lover's treat. There's a wonderful taster menu of updated Roman cuisine and some very interesting wines. ⓐ Via Giuseppe Gioacchino Belli 59–61 ☎ 06 3210992 🌐 www.ristorantelarcangelo.it 🕒 13.00–14.30, 20.00–23.30 Mon–Fri, 20.00–23.30 Sat, closed Sun 🚍 Bus: 30, 70, 49, 87, 186, 280, 913

Monti, Esquilino & Quirinale

The Italian president's residence stands loftily atop the Quirinal Hill. East of here is the Monti neighbourhood, an unspoilt and unpretentious area that has a local, village atmosphere and feel, and further east is the Esquilino, a chaotic area often overlooked by tourists that centres on Piazza Vittorio Emanuele II and is known for its thriving immigrant community.

SIGHTS & ATTRACTIONS

Fontana di Trevi (Trevi Fountain)

The most famous of Rome's fountains is the work of Nicolò Salvi, who took it over in 1732 – more than a century after the project was abandoned by Bernini – and of Gianpaolo Pannini, who completed it in 1762. Its name is thought to derive from the *tre vie* (three roads) which converge here, and it is the fountainhead of the Acqua Vergine aqueduct, which has brought water to this site since 19 BC. Neptune, at the centre, is flanked by Tritons, one struggling to control his horse, symbolising stormy seas, while his conch-blowing companion represents the ocean in repose. In the niches on either side of Neptune are Health and Abundance, and above are the Four Seasons. People throw coins over their shoulder into the fountain to ensure a speedy return to Rome (see also page 41). ➌ Piazza Fontana di Trevi Ⓝ Bus: 52, 53, 61, 62, 71, 80, 95, 116, 119, 175, 492, 590, 630; Metro: Barberini

Palazzo del Quirinale

Former summer retreat of the popes, and, from 1870 to 1944, seat of the kings of Italy, the Quirinale Palace is now the presidential

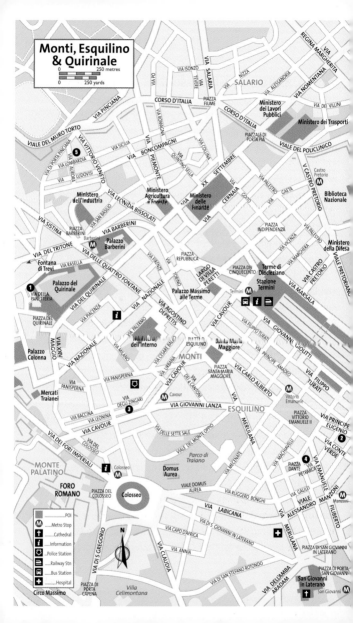

Monti, Esquilino & Quirinale

0   250 metres
0   250 yards

VIA ISONZO
VIA NIZZA
VIA SALARIA
VIA TEVERE
SALARIO
REGINA MARGHERITA
VIA NOMENTANA
CORSO D'ITALIA
PIAZZA FIUME
VIA ALESSANDRIA
VIA DEI VILLINI
VIA PINCIANA
CORSO D'ITALIA
Ministero dei Lavori Pubblici
Ministero dei Trasporti
VIALE DEL MURO TORTO
VIA DI PORTA PINCIANA
VIA VITTORIO VENETO
VIA SICILIA
VIA ROMAGNA
VIA BONCOMPAGNI
VIA PIEMONTE
VIA COLLINA
PIAZZALE DI PORTA PIA
VIALE DEL POLICLINICO
5
VIA LOMBARDIA
VIA (LUDOVISI)
VIA LEONIDA BISSOLATI
VIA QUINTINO SELLA
XX SETTEMBRE
VIA SAN BASILIO
Ministero dell'Industria
Ministero Agricoltura e Foreste
Ministero delle Finanze
VIA CERNAIA
VIA GOITO
VIA PALESTRO
GAETA
V. CASTRO PRETORIO
Castro Pretorio
Biblioteca Nazionale
VIA SISTINA
PIAZZA BARBERINI
VIA BARBERINI
VIA
PIAZZA INDIPENDENZA
VIA PALESTRO
VIA VICENZA
Ministero della Difesa
Barberini
VIA DEL TRITONE
Palazzo Barberini
VIA DELLE QUATTRO FONTANE
VIA FIRENZE
PIAZZA REPUBBLICA
PIAZZA DEI CINQUECENTO
Terme di Diocleziano
VIA MARGHERA
VIA CASTRO PRETORIO
VIALE PRETORIANO
Fontana di Trevi
VIA RASELLA
PIAZZA BARBERINI
Palazzo del Quirinale
VIA DEL QUIRINALE
PRINI
LARGO DI VILLA PERETTI
Stazione Termini
VIA MARSALA
1
VIA DELLA PANETTERIA
VIA PIACENZA
VIA NAZIONALE
VIA AGOSTINO DEPRETIS
Palazzo Massimo alle Terme
Termini
VIA CAVOUR
VIA FILIPPO TURATI
VIA GIOVANNI GIOLITTI
PIAZZA DEL QUIRINALE
i
VIA PALERMO
PIAZZA DELL'ESQUILINO
Santa Maria Maggiore
VIA PRINCIPE AMEDEO
VIA FILIPPO TURATI
Palazzo Colonna
VIA XXIV MAGGIO
VIA NAZIONALE
VIA MILANO
Ministero dell'Interno
PIAZZA ESQUILINO
MONTI
VIA CARLO ALBERTO
Mercati Traianei
VIA PANISPERNA
VIA URBANA
VIA CESARE BALBO
VIA PANISPERNA
PIAZZA SANTA MARIA MAGGIORE
Vittorio Emanuele
VIA PRINCIPE EUGENIO
VIA DEGLI ZINGARI
VIA CAVOUR
VIA G. LANZINI
3
Cavour
VIA GIOVANNI LANZA
ESQUILINO
PIAZZA VITTORIO EMANUELE II
VIA CONTE VERDE
VIA BACCINA
VIA LEONINA
VIA DELLE SETTE SALE
NERULANA
VIA MACHIAVELLI
4
VIA CAVOUR
VIALE DEL MONTE OPPIO
VIA DANTE
VIA EMANUEL
VIA DEI FORI IMPERIALI
VIA DEL COLOSSEO
Parco di Traiano
VIA PETRARCA
VIA GALILEI
MONTE PALATINO
i
Colosseo
Domus Aurea
VIA MECENATE
VIALE ALESSANDRO MANZONI
Manzoni
FORO ROMANO
PIAZZA DEL COLOSSEO
Colosseo
VIALE DOMUS AUREA
VIA RUGGERO BONGHI
MERULANA
VIA LABICANA
PIAZZA DI SAN GIOVANNI IN LATERANO
VIA CAPO D'AFRICA
VIA DI S. GIOVANNI IN LATERANO
VIA DELL'AMBA ARADAM
VIA ANNIA
VIA CLAUDIA
PIAZZA DI PORTA SAN GIOVANNI
VIA DI SAN STEFANO ROTONDO
San Giovanni in Laterano
San Giovanni
VIA DI S GREGORIO
N
Villa Celimontana
PIAZZA DI PORTA CAPENA
Circo Massimo

Legend

- ....POI
- M ....Metro Stop
- † ....Cathedral
- i ....Information
- 🚓 ....Police Station
- 🚂 ....Railway Stn
- 🚌 ....Bus Station
- ✚ ....Hospital

residence. Pope Gregory XIII (1572–85) first chose this site as an escape from the fetid summer conditions of the Vatican. Many illustrious architects have had a hand in its design, Bernini among them. He was responsible for the Benediction Loggia (1638) over the main entrance in Piazza del Quirinale and the *manica lunga* (long sleeve), a long, narrow wing running along the Via del Quirinale in which the pope housed his family. Classical music concerts are held on Sundays from September to June in the Cappella Paolina.
🅐 Piazza del Quirinale 🅣 06 46991 🅦 www.quirinale.it
🅛 08.30–12.00 Sun (early Sept–mid-July); closed certain Sundays (call to check first); closed Mon–Sat 🅐 Bus: H, 40, 60, 64, 70, 71, 117, 170; Metro: Barberini 🅘 Admission charge

San Giovanni in Laterano

Rome's main cathedral church, this is the pope's titular seat as Bishop of Rome. Alessandro Galilei's dramatic entrance façade of 1735 is crowned by gigantic statues of Christ, John the Baptist, John the Evangelist and the 12 Doctors of the Church. The central bronze doors come from the ancient Senate House in the Foro Romano.

Emperor Constantine built the first church here (314–18) over army barracks in a palace that then stood on the site. The Vandals, earthquakes and fire destroyed this and later churches, after which, in 1586, the core of what can now be seen was begun. Borromini was responsible for the interior (1646).

The church retains its original basilican shape; within, there is a Gothic tabernacle (1367) over the high altar (at which only the pope can say Mass), accompanied by a wooden table said to have been used by St Peter and the earliest popes. The relics venerated are allegedly the skulls of St Peter and St Paul. San Giovanni's 13th century cloisters are remarkable for their twisted columns and their Cosmati decoration, but the most interesting feature of the whole complex is the Baptistery, dating from 432 and the only part of the earliest church to have survived.

Its design and plan – a vaulted octagon – provided the model for all subsequent baptisteries throughout Italy. ⓐ Piazza di San Giovanni in Laterano 4 ⓣ 06 69886433 ⓒ Church: daily 07.00–18.30; Baptistery: daily 07.00–12.30, 16.00–19.00 ⓝ Bus: 16, 81, 85, 87, 117, 186, 218, 571, 650, 714, 850; Tram: 3; Metro: San Giovanni

Santa Maria Maggiore

The Baroque façade on Via Cavour is the work of Ferdinando Fuga (1740) but it frames an early Christian basilica. The main entrance, facing Piazza Santa Maria Maggiore, built for Pope Clement X (1670–76), has a deep-arched loggia where heretical books were burnt in the Virgin's honour. In front is a column from the Basilica of Maxentius (in the Foro Romano), topped with a statue of the Virgin, balanced at the rear by an Egyptian obelisk placed there in 1587. The vast nave with 40 ancient columns is part of the 5th-century building, though the decorated pavement is medieval, as is the bell

ⓞ *The beautiful ceiling at Santa Maria Maggiore*

tower (the tallest in Rome). Best of all are the 5th-century mosaics in the architrave (36 scenes from the Old Testament) and those on the triumphal arch above the altar. In the apse is Jacopo Torriti's mosaic *The Coronation of the Virgin* (1275). The Cappella Sistina, built for Sixtus V (1585–90), is filled with precious marbles looted from Rome's ancient monuments. ⓐ Piazza Santa Maria Maggiore ☎ 06 69886800 ⏱ daily 07.00–19.00 🚍 Bus: H, 16, 70, 75, 84, 105, 360, 590, 649; Tram: 5, 14; Metro: Cavour or Termini

CULTURE

Galleria Nazionale d'Arte Antica: Palazzo Barberini
(National Gallery of Ancient Art: Barberini Palace)

The Palazzo Barberini (1625–33) was built by Carlo Maderno with the help of Borromini, and completed by Bernini for the powerful Barberini family. Part of the family collection is still housed here, but this – along with the building and the rest of the contents – now belongs to the state.

The palace's most important room is the Gran Salone, whose centrepiece is Pietro da Cortona's ceiling painting *The Allegory of Divine Providence* (1638–9), which celebrates the virtues of Pope Urban VIII for whom it was painted. Italian painting of the 13th to 16th centuries is well represented, with works by Fra Angelico, Perugino, Filippo Lippi, Lorenzo Lotto and Andrea del Sarto. Most famous of all is Raphael's *La Fornarina* (thought to be a portrait of his mistress). There are also works by Bronzino, Caravaggio and Canaletto, and a portrait of England's King Henry VIII by Holbein. ⓐ Via delle Quattro Fontane 13 ☎ 06 4824184 and ☎ 06 32810 (for tickets) ⏱ 08.30–19.30 Tues–Sun, closed Mon 🚍 Bus: 52, 53, 61, 63, 80, 95, 116, 175, 492, 630; Metro: Barberini ❶ Admission charge

Palazzo Massimo alle Terme

The Palazzo Massimo (part of the Museo Nazionale Romano, see below) houses Roman paintings, mosaics, sculpture, coins and antiquities, many of which were found on the sites of Ancient Roman villas in and around the city, some of the most remarkable on the grounds of the Villa Farnesina in Trastevere. ⓐ Largo di Villa Peretti 1 ❶ 06 39967700 ❷ 09.00–19.45 Tues–Sun, closed Mon ❽ Bus: 30, 70, 81, 87, 116, 130, 186, 492, 628 ❶ Admission charge (the entrance ticket allows entry into all four Museo Nazionale Romano sites and is valid for three days)

Terme di Diocleziano (Baths of Diocletian)

The Museo Nazionale Romano is one of Rome's most important museums of antiquities and one of the world's leading repositories of classical art. Before the Jubilee in 2000, the collection was split and

🔺 *The Trevi Fountain in Piazza di Trevi: the most famous fountain in Rome*

rehoused at four renovated locations, including this, original, location (the other three are the Palazzo Massimo alle Terme, see opposite, Palazzo Altemps, see page 82, and Crypta Balbi). To get an idea of the interior of Ancient Rome's baths, visit Santa Maria degli Angeli and the Museo Nazionale Romano, both within the 4th-century Baths of Diocletian. Originally, the complex covered over a hectare (2½ acres) of ground between the present Piazza dei Cinquecento and Piazza della Repubblica and could accommodate more than 3,000 people. The shape of an attached stadium can still be traced in the curve of two 19th-century buildings forming the southwestern perimeter of Piazza della Repubblica (just southwest of the museum). It provides a remarkable setting for sculpture, mosaics and frescoes, which lined the cloisters of a convent built by Michelangelo, and the largest chunks of surviving baths. ⓐ Viale Enrico de Nicola 79 (information and public transport are the same as for Palazzo Massimo alle Terme above)

RETAIL THERAPY

MAS This is the oldest department store in Rome. Crammed to the rafters, it is a (patient) bargain-hunter's dream. ⓐ Piazza Vittorio Emanuele 138 ⓣ 06 4466078 ⓦ www.magazziniallostatuto.com ⓛ 09.00–13.00, 15.45–19.45 Mon–Sat, closed Sun ⓝ Bus: 30, 40, 44, 46, 62, 63, 64, 70, 81, 85, 87, 95, 117, 170, 175, 492, 628, 780, 810, 850

Panella High-end bakery Panella (subtitle: The art of bread) sells mouthwatering pizza by the slice, regional breads, sweet rolls and cakes. They also make cakes to Ancient Roman recipes and decorative breads for parties. ⓐ Via Merulana 54–55 ⓣ 06 4872344 ⓛ 08.00–14.00, 17.00–20.00 Mon–Wed, Fri & Sat, 08.00–14.00 Thur, closed Sun ⓝ Bus: 16, 87, 571, 714; Metro: Vittorio Emanuele

TAKING A BREAK

Il Gelato di San Crispino £ ❶ An ice-cream lover's paradise. Flavours include cinnamon and ginger, and liquorice. ⓐ Via della Panetteria 42 ❶ 06 6793924 ⓦ www.ilgelatodisancrispino.com ⓛ 12.00–00.30 Sun–Thur, 12.00–01.30 Fri & Sat, closed Tues (winter) ⓝ Bus: 52, 53, 61, 62, 71, 80, 95, 116, 119, 175, 492, 590, 630; Metro: Barberini

Palazzo del Freddo di Giovanni Fassi £ ❷ An old-fashioned ice-cream parlour producing its *gelato* in-house since 1880. ⓐ Via Principe Eugenio 65 ❶ 06 4464740 ⓦ www.palazzodelfreddo.it ⓝ Bus: 105, 150, 360, 590, 649; Tram: 5, 14; Metro: Vittorio Emanuele

AFTER DARK

Vecchia Roma £ ❸ A real find – pizzas with imaginative toppings. ⓐ Via Leonina 10 ❶ 06 4745887 ⓛ daily 12.30–14.30, 19.00–23.00 ⓝ Bus: 3, 8, 75, 85, 87, 117, 186; Metro: Cavour

Danilo £–££ ❹ A family-run trattoria that serves seasonal classics. The wine list is excellent. ⓐ Via Petrarca 13 ❶ 06 77200111 ⓦ www.trattoriadadanilo.it ⓛ 12.30–15.00, 19.00–23.00 Mon–Sat, closed Sun ⓝ Bus: 87, 360, 590, 810; Tram: 3; Metro: Vittorio Emanuele or Manzoni

Aurora 10 da Pino il Sommelier ££ ❺ Known for its 250 varieties of wine from all over Italy and for its excellent fish and seafood. ⓐ Via Aurora 10 ❶ 06 4742779 ⓦ www.aurora10.it ⓛ 12.00–15.00, 19.00–23.00 Tues–Sun, closed Mon ⓝ Bus: 62, 175, 492, 590; Metro: Barberini

ⓞ *The Villa d'Este in Tivoli is a spectacular sight*

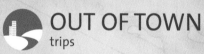

OUT OF TOWN
trips

Tivoli

Located 40 km (25 miles) from Rome, hilltop Tivoli, with its ideal position on the Aniene River, is both a proverbial and literal breath of fresh air from the noise and fumes of the capital. This was not something that was sniffed at even in ancient times, when the Romans used the area to escape the stifling heat of summer. During Renaissance times, too, some of the city's most prominent citizens built spectacular villas here. Today Tivoli largely makes its living from the quarrying and export of the local travertine rock, as any visitor will see if they drive the SS5 route from Rome to here.

The main attractions for visitors to Tivoli today are its three UNESCO World Heritage Sites: Villa Adriana, Villa d'Este and Villa Gregoriana. In order to take in everything you will need plenty of time, so either set out early on the day of your visit, or stay overnight in one of the small hotels. Tourist Office Azienda Autonoma di Turismo ⓐ Largo Garibaldi ❶ 0774 334522 ⓒ 09.00–13.00, 15.00–17.00 Mon–Fri, 09.00–19.00 Sat, closed Sun

GETTING THERE

By rail

Local trains connect Rome's Tiburtina Station with Tivoli with a journey time of about 45 minutes. There is a shuttle bus service from the station to the town centre and Villa d'Este. See **Trenitalia** (❶ 89 20 21 ⓦ www.ferroviedellostato.it).

By road

COTRAL buses (❶ 800 174471 ⓦ www.cotralspa.it) leave Rome for Tivoli every 20 minutes from the terminal on the Ponte Mammolo

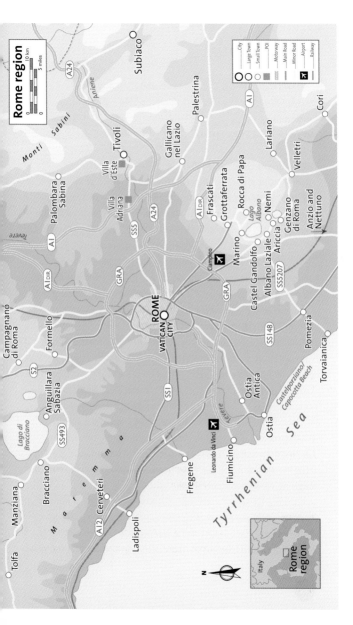

stop, on metro line B. The trip takes about an hour. There is a shuttle bus service from Tivoli's main square to Villa Adriana.

SIGHTS & ATTRACTIONS

Villa Adriana (Hadrian's Villa)

Tivoli's main attraction, just outside the town, is the Villa Adriana (Hadrian's Villa), built by the emperor between AD 118 and 134. Hadrian loved to experiment with architecture (much of the Pantheon can be attributed to his designer's eye) and his villa is no exception, with walkways, water features and colonnades.

Much of the site is now in ruins, but it still makes for an evocative and relaxing visit, strolling the ponds and gardens, and trying to re-create in one's mind what was once one of the most stunning villas of the imperial age. Sadly, the main palace buildings are the least recognisable, but other areas of the complex clearly illustrate the influences Hadrian brought back with him from Greece and Egypt. The massive Pecile through which you enter, for example, is a reproduction of a building in Athens. One of the loveliest parts of the complex, the Canopus, is a copy of the sanctuary of Serapis near Alexandria, with its long strip of water decorated on either side by columns and statues.

Like so much of the area in and around Rome, the wealth of history means that archaeologists are constantly uncovering more and more treasures. A small museum near the Canopus gives some insight into the relics that have been excavated here and the ongoing work to discover more.

Among the other ruins that still evoke their original purpose are two bath complexes, a *cryptoporticus* (underground passageway) adorned with the autographs of visiting artists from the Renaissance and Baroque periods, including Bernini, and the Teatro

◆ *The Villa Adriana is an architectural beauty*

Marittimo (Maritime Theatre). A circular brick wall here, 45 m (148 ft) in diameter, encloses a moat beyond which is an island of columns and a *domus* (little villa), complete with its own baths, bedrooms and gardens. The bridge across the moat today is made of cement, but the original would have been a wooden pathway that could be hauled up for extra privacy. It is the place to which it is believed that Hadrian retired at siesta time in order to be alone.

VILLA D'ESTE

Another important sight in Tivoli is the Villa d'Este, a lavish palace built over the ruins of a Benedictine monastery in 1550 for Cardinal Ippolito d'Este, son of Lucretia Borgia. The cardinal wanted a residence every bit as spectacular as Hadrian's had been – and he got one. The brilliant frescoes by Correggio, Da Volterra and Perin del Vaga in its seven rooms depicting scenes from the history of the d'Este family in Tivoli are certainly worth seeing if you're an art lover. But the real highlight, and what draws most visitors, is the gardens, which many consider to be the most attractive in Italy. Tiered and landscaped, and made up of manicured lawns and shrubbery, the grounds are dotted with some 51 fountains, including the Fontana del Bicchierone, designed by the great Baroque sculptor Bernini, and a hydraulic fountain whose mechanism emulates the sound of music. If you were ever in doubt as to the extravagance of wealthy Renaissance families, the Villa d'Este should put you right. ⓐ Piazza Trento 1 ① 0774 312070 ⓦ www.villadestetivoli.info ⓒ 09.00–1 hour before sunset Tues–Sun, closed Mon ① Admission charge

Despite the grandeur and ambition of the project, Hadrian only enjoyed his retirement villa for three years before his death in AD 138. After the fall of the Roman Empire, it fell into the hands of looters and treasure hunters, who sold their finds to museums all over the world. Marble and mosaic finds from here now make up a large proportion of the collections of Roman art at the Musei Capitolini (see page 75).

ⓐ Via di Villa Adriana ❶ 0774 530203 ⓦ www.villa-adriana.net
🕒 daily 09.00–1 hour before sunset ❶ Admission charge

🔺 Villa d'Este's water features rival any today

Villa Gregoriana

Villa Gregoriana is a park with an impressive 100-m (330-ft) waterfall created in 1831, when Pope Gregory XVI redirected the River Aniene to prevent it flooding Tivoli. It was a popular stop on any Italian Grand Tour as paintings from that period attest. After being closed for many years, the park reopened in 2005 and boasts lush scenery and dramatic views from its many pathways. ⓐ Piazza Tempio di Vesta ❶ 0774 382733 Ⓦ www.villagregoriana.it ⏱ 10.00–18.30 Tues–Sun, closed Mon (Apr–mid-Oct); 10.00–14.30 Mon–Sat, 10.00–16.00 Sun (mid-Oct–Nov & Mar)

TAKING A BREAK

Adriano ££ Across from the entrance to Villa Adriano, the better-than-average menu here includes tasty home-made pasta, and there's also a well-kept garden for alfresco dining. The Adriano's on-site inn also offers ten elegant guest rooms. ⓐ Largo M Yourcenar 2 ❶ 0774 382235 Ⓦ www.hoteladriano.it ⏱ 12.30–16.00, 19.30–23.00 daily

ACCOMMODATION

B&B Luigia £ A small, unpretentious bed and breakfast, with on-site restaurant, located 3 km (2 miles) from Tivoli centre. ⓐ Via Villa Adriana 186 ❶ 0774 531441 or ❶ 339 4291762

Hotel Le Rose £ Simple, clean rooms with full amenities, and a restaurant offering typical Italian cooking. Near railway and bus stations and near thermal baths. ⓐ Via Tiburtina 256 ❶ 0774 357930 Ⓦ www.lerosehotel.it

Ostia & Ostia Antica

Visitors to the ruins of Ostia Antica need to make a few preparations to maximise their enjoyment of what will be a thrilling experience: the harbour area of Ancient Rome contains some archaeological features that are tremendously evocative of how vivid this part of the city must once have been. Comfortable walking shoes are imperative, and it's a good idea to avoid scheduling your exploration for the hottest part of the day. Whenever you come, do bring your own bottled water – to guard against both the heat and the exorbitant prices charged by local vendors!

GETTING THERE

By rail
Take the Roma-Lido train from the Roma Porta San Paolo Station (next door to the Piramide metro stop). Departures are every 10 minutes, and the trip takes 20 minutes.

By road
Follow Via del Mare southwest, which leads directly from Rome to Ostia, with a journey time of around 40 minutes. Avoid driving on summer weekends when Romans head en masse to the beach.

SIGHTS & ATTRACTIONS

Ostia Antica
Situated on the Tyrrhenian coast, Ostia Antica was a vital trading port in the days of the Roman Empire, and home to a motley crew of sailors and wealthy merchants. Much of the riches of the empire

depended on the ability to import and export between the Mediterranean and North Africa, and the vast 2nd-century *horrea* (warehouses) were built to house grain shipments. However, when the course of the River Tiber changed, the port became silted up and the once-prosperous city was abandoned to the elements. This may have affected the way of life in the early millennium, but the sand covering was a saving grace for 20th-century archaeologists engaged in the extensive Scavi di Ostia Antica (Ostia Antica excavations) that revealed the mysteries of this ancient area.

Before starting your explorations of the ruins take a look around the lovely medieval *borgo* (old town) and the impressive Castello delle Rovere, accessed via the footbridge from the train station. It was built by Pope Julius in 1483 when he was Cardinal of Ostia Antica. Inside are faded frescoes, reportedly completed by Baldassare Peruzzi, a student of Michelangelo.

The main street of Ostia Antica is the Decumanus Maximus, which leads past the Terme di Nettuno (Baths of Neptune), from which there is a good view of the polychrome mosaic pavements depicting Neptune and Amphitrite. Behind the baths was a fire department, which filtered water from the harbour whenever the vital warehouses were at risk. The commercial centre is known as Piazza delle Corporazioni where ground-floor shops and offices can still be identified by the mosaics depicting individual trades: grain merchant, ship-fitter, rope-maker and so forth. On one side of the square, the beautiful *teatro* (theatre) was built by Agrippa, and restored by Rome city council in the 20th century so that it could continue to stage open-air performances.

Many of the former residences and temples can still be made out, despite their ruined status. The Domus di Apuleio (House of Apulius) was built in low-level Pompeian style with few windows; the Casa di

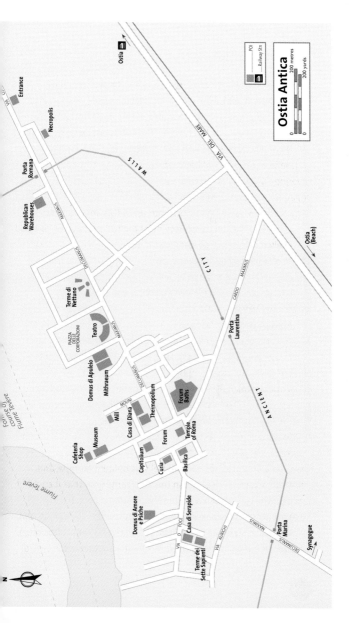

LIDO DI OSTIA

Romans are ever in search of places to escape from the summer heat and this coastal town was created in the 1930s for just that purpose. It is commonly referred to as Ostia Moderna (New Ostia) to differentiate it from the ruins of Ostia Antica, and is reached from Rome by the Via Cristoforo Colombo near the Baths of Caracalla.

However, not only is this stretch of beach heaving with crowds in summer, the water and the coastline leave a lot to be desired in terms of cleanliness. Far better options are at Torvaianica, 11 km (7 miles) south of Ostia, which pays more attention to the state of the environment, as does the Castelporziano/Capocotta beach between Ostia and Torvaianica. In addition there's a nature reserve across the street from the beach, which means that your sunbathing scenery consists of sea on one side and sand dunes on the other.

On the Lido itself there are beach cafés and restaurants as well as a gay section, *Il Buco* (the hole), to which gays and lesbians flock from June to September, and a nudist section signposted *Oasi Naturista di Capocotta*. The nudist section of the beach has the best restaurants.

Diana (House of Diana) clearly shows several rooms surrounding a courtyard, as does the Domus di Amore e Psiche (House of Cupid and Psyche), which also has a well-preserved marbled floor. The Casa di Serapide (House of Serapis) is a 2nd-century multilevel dwelling, while one street further along are *insulae* (apartment buildings) that provided housing for a large majority of Ostia's population.

One of the most fascinating remains, if only because it illustrates how little has changed between ancient and modern times, is the *thermopolium* (bar), a Roman café complete with seats outside and a fresco indicating the menu on offer.

North of the House of Diana is the museum, which houses numerous items excavated from the site, including frescoes that illustrate daily life in Ostia in ancient times, along with elegant sarcophagi and a statue of *Mithras Slaying the Bull* from one of Ostia's *mithraea*. West of the museum is the Forum where the city's most important temple (dedicated to Jupiter, Juno and Minerva) was located, as well as thermal baths, a basilica (which in Roman times was a secular hall of justice) and smaller temples. Continue on down the main street, and to the right you'll see some of the ancient warehouses that have been wonderfully preserved.

The Terme dei Sette Sapienti (Baths of the Seven Wise Men) are named after a collection of rather suggestive frescoes that were excavated from the site. The Porta Marina leads to what was once the seashore.

To the south of the port are the ruins of the synagogue, considered to be one of the oldest in the Western world. ⓐ Viale dei Romagnoli 717 ⓞ 06 56352830 ⓦ www.ostiaantica.net ⓛ 08.30–1 hour before sunset Tues–Sun, closed Mon ⓘ Admission charge

TAKING A BREAK

The best seafood restaurants can be found on the Castelporziano/Capocotta beach between Ostia and Torvaianica, particularly along the nudist section. The museum at the excavations has a cafeteria that serves breakfasts and light lunches.

🔺 *Imagine the hustle and bustle of Ostia Antica in Roman times*

La Vecchia Pineta £££ A memorable and atmospheric restaurant with gourmet fare, the freshest fish and seafood and a sea view. ⓐ Piazza dell'Acquilone 4 ⓣ 06 5647 ⓛ daily 12.30–16.00, 19.30–23.00

ACCOMMODATION

Agli Scavi di Ostia Antica £ This small villa is only 100 m (330 ft) from the entrance to the excavations. All rooms look out on to a garden and have en-suite bathrooms and air conditioning. Breakfast is included. ⓐ Via della Stazione di Ostia Antica 7 ⓣ 06 5657308 ⓦ www.ostiaantica.net/bandb

Ostia Antica Park Hotel ££–£££ Conveniently situated 80-room hotel with modern design, a restaurant and a nice spa. ⓐ Viale dei Romagnoli 1041a ⓣ 06 5652089 ⓦ www.ostiaanticaparkhotel.it

Bracciano & Cerveteri

Lago di Bracciano (Lake Bracciano) is the closest of northern Lazio's lakes to the city, formed by an extinct volcanic crater. Along with the beaches around Ostia, it is a favourite summer escape for Romans, particularly avid anglers, and is only an hour by train from the city. Even if you don't want to try your hand with rod and line yourself, the restaurants surrounding the lake offer excellent freshly caught catch of the day.

The town of Cerveteri is not much to look at, but the necropolis just outside the town provides the most accessible Etruscan ruins in the area. The Necropoli della Bandicaccia were declared a UNESCO World Heritage Site in 2004, together with the necropolis in Tarquinia (about 50 km (31 miles) northwest of Cerveteri). There has been a settlement here since the 10th century BC when it was an important trade centre.

GETTING THERE

By rail

Trains for Bracciano depart from Rome's Ostiense Station, and the journey time is around an hour. Take the train that goes in the direction of Viterbo.

By road

Cerveteri is 30 km (19 miles) northwest of Rome. The best way to reach the town is by bus, as the railway station is at Ladispoli, 7 km (4 1/3 miles) from the centre. Buses depart from Rome's Lepanto metro station, line A, more or less every 30 minutes, arriving at Cerveteri's Piazza Aldo Moro. The trip takes 1 hour 20 minutes.

◆ *The town of Bracciano sits on the western shore of the lake*

○ *One of the streets of the necropolis*

SIGHTS & ATTRACTIONS

Bracciano

Lago di Bracciano's main settlement is the town of Bracciano on the western shore. Towering over it is the Castello Orsini-Odescalchi (ⓐ Piazza Mazzini 14 ⓘ 06 99804348 ⓦ www.odescalchi.it), a late 15th-century castle. While the castle's outer walls are largely in ruins, the interior houses some historical suits of armour and frescoes, and the view from the ramparts is beautiful. It recently acquired fame as the place where Tom Cruise married Katie Holmes.

The best beach for swimming is on Via Argenti to the south of the town. You can rent a boat to mess about on the water, then refresh yourself in the nearby *trattorie*.

Cerveteri

Cerveteri, the Roman Caere, was a large and financially profitable city during the Etruscan era, benefiting particularly from trading links with Greece. Its wealth derived largely from the mineral riches of the Tolfa Hills to the northeast. At one time the town spread over 8 km (5 miles), 30 times its present size, controlling territory that stretched for 50 km (31 miles). The city, along with other Etruscan territories, went into decline around 351 BC when the Romans took control of much of the area.

CULTURE

Museo Nazionale Cerite

Many of Cerveteri's archaeological finds have been removed to larger museums around the world, but the 16th-century Castello Raspoli in the centre of the old town has four large rooms

containing some of the items that were excavated from the necropolis, including vases, sarcophagi, terracotta pots and other everyday objects from the Etruscan period. ⓐ Piazza Santa Maria, Cerveteri ⓣ 06 9941354 ⓛ 08.30–19.30 Tues–Sun, closed Mon

Necropolis & Museum

Most of Cerveteri dates from medieval times, but the necropolis, 1 km (²/₃ mile) outside town, is a reminder that the area was important to the Etruscans. The ruins of this 'city of the dead' show the streets that meandered between tombs and burial chambers from the 7th to the 1st centuries BC. The male dead were buried in stone sarcophagi, accompanied by the cremated ashes of their slaves, while women were interred in separate burial chambers. Today you can see 12 tombs between the two roads that bisect the city. Among them are the Tomba dei Letti Funebri (Tombs of the Funeral Beds), the Tomba degli Scudi e delle Sedie (Tombs of the Shields and Chairs), which consists of separate rooms linked by hallways, and the Tomba dei Rilievi (Tomb of the Reliefs), decorated with carvings. ⓣ 06 9940001 ⓛ 08.30–1 hour before sunset Tues–Sun, closed Mon ⓘ Admission charge

TAKING A BREAK

Gooh £ Modern café and restaurant serving local specialities (including breakfast). ⓐ Via Passo di Palo 111, Cerveteri ⓣ 06 9940672 ⓦ www.gooh.it ⓛ 06.30–16.00, 19.30–23.00 Tues–Sun, closed Mon

The Castelli Romani & around

Beyond the suburbs of Rome the 13 towns that make up the Castelli
Romani area (see map page 119) were the place of choice for
summer villas during the Roman Empire as well as castle-building
during the Middle Ages, when the surrounding hills, the Colli Albani,
were the summer playground for the rich and powerful. The best
towns to visit on a short trip from Rome are Frascati and
Grottaferrata, east of Lago Albano to the Monte Cavo and Rocca di
Papa, and west of Lago Albano to the towns of Albano Laziale and
Castel Gandolfo. The area south of Lago Albano – the towns of
Genzano di Roma, Nemi and Velletri – also makes a good visit. Wine
lovers in particular should sample the local grapes at the many
wineries, but even if you're just after a day trip to escape the hectic
lifestyle of the city the area is only 20 minutes' drive from Rome and
makes for a refreshing break.

○ *The beautiful view over Lago Albano*

GETTING THERE

By rail

A small railway line runs from Rome's Termini Station into the Alban
Hills. Some services stop at Frascati, others continue to Albano
Laziale, via Marino and Castel Gandolfo. Services are infrequent,
however, so check the timetables in the station or at the tourist
office. Tickets can be bought at any newsstand at Termini Station,
but you'd be advised to buy a return (*andata e ritorno*), as the
provincial stations are often unstaffed. The rail journey is very
scenic, passing Rome's aqueducts, vineyards and market gardens
before skirting Lake Albano.

By road

COTRAL buses (📞 800 174471 🌐 www.cotralspa.it) leave Rome every 30
minutes from the terminus above the metro station Anagnina, line A.

Despite the scenic rail trip, without question the best way to see
the Castelli Romani is by car. You will be able to see more, and
travelling at your own pace will enable you to get to the heart of
this interesting and appealing area.

Coming from the A1 motorway Milan–Rome at the Fiano
Romano junction, follow directions to Roma Nord. Once on the GRA,
exit at the 21–22 Tuscolana Anagnina junction and follow the signs
for the various towns in the region.

SIGHTS & ATTRACTIONS

Castel Gandolfo & west of Lago Albano

Even the pope feels the need to escape the beating summer sun
and retreats, via the ancient Via Appia, to his summer residence

Castel Gandolfo. Named after the castle owned by the powerful 12th-century Genoese Gandolfo family, the fortress towers 400 m (1,312 ft) above Lago Albano. Between July and September the Papal Address every Sunday at midday moves from St Peter's Basilica in the Vatican to the balcony of this far cooler option.

From Castel Gandolfo a panoramic road leads to Albano Laziale, one of the nicest towns along the Via Appia. The town's Piazza Mazzina looks south to the Villa Communale park with the partial remains of a villa that once belonged to Pomeroy. Along the main street, Corso Mattrotti, the church of San Pietro was built over the foundations of the baths of a Roman garrison. Near the church of Santa Maria della Stella is a small museum housing an archaeological collection of Etruscan and Roman artefacts that were found in the town. On Via della Stella is the Tomb of Horatii and the Curiatii, with buildings dating from Rome's Republican era.
ⓦ www.museicivicialbano.it ⓛ Museo Civico 09.00–13.00 Fri–Tues, 09.00–13.00, 16.00–19.00 Wed & Thur ⓘ Admission charge

South of Lago Albano
Genzano, 2 km (1¼ miles) further on from Albano Laziale, has a pleasant medieval centre built around the Piazza Frasconi. A road from here leads along to Lago Albano's crater and sweeps down to the shore through dense woods. Try to visit in June when the road down from the main square is covered in flowers to celebrate Corpus Domini.

A detour east will take you to Nemi. Built high above a tiny crater lake of the same name, the village itself is not really worthy of a visit but the lake shore is a wonderful spot for a picnic. Again, try to visit the area in June when on the first Sunday there is a strawberry festival in the town of Genzano to celebrate its most famous product.

> ### MONTE CAVO & ROCCA DI PAPA
> On the eastern side of Lago Albano the Via dei Laghi leads to the summit of the 949-m (3,114-ft) high Monte Cavo, which was once home to a convent and a temple to Jupiter. From here there is a road to the highest of the hilltop towns, Rocca di Papa, which is worth the winding trip to see the attractive old quarter dating from the Middle Ages.

On the northern side of the lake is a local museum, containing scale models of two pleasure boats said to have been built by that most infamous of emperors, Caligula. The original boats, like the empire, did not survive intact and sank to the bottom of the lake, but they were raised in the 1930s under the orders of Mussolini – hence the typically Fascist-style buildings in which they are now housed. Unfortunately, the boats were set on fire during the final days of the German Occupation, but these models offer powerful insight into ancient shipbuilding skills.

ⓐ Museo delle Navi Romane: Nemi a Via di Diana 13 🕓 09.00–19.00 Mon–Sat, 09.00–13.00 Sun (summer); 09.00–17.00 Mon–Sat, 09.00–13.00 Sun (winter) ⓘ Admission charge

Frascati & around
Frascati, 20 km (12 miles) from Rome, is one of the most beautiful as well as the most famous of the Castelli Romani towns. The majestic, privately owned, Villa Aldobrandini, built by Giacomo della Porta in 1598, dominates the town, and the gardens, which offer wonderful views across the region all the way to Rome, are open to the public.

Frascati is best known for its production of the eponymous dry white wine, and many wineries (*cantine*) in the region offer tours and tastings. Check at the tourist office for days and times.

🔺 *The majestic Villa Aldobrandini is the nexus of Frascati*

Approximately 3 km (2 miles) from Frascati is the medieval town of **Grottaferrata**, known both for its wine production and for its 11th-century Abbey of St Nilo (ⓦ www.abbaziagreca.it). The abbey's gorgeous Byzantine interior is decorated with 13th-century mosaics. In the small Farnesian chapel are 17th-century frescoes by Domenichino. The town also has a small museum (🕒 09.00–12.00, 15.30–18.30 daily; closed for restoration at the time of writing), which will appeal to art lovers with exhibits of classical and medieval sculpture. Frascati Tourist Office ⓐ Piazza Marconi 1 ⓣ 06 9420331

TAKING A BREAK

Antico Ristorante Pagnanelli £££ This elegant restaurant, overlooking Lake Albano, has been in operation since 1882. Fish is a speciality, as is the home-made ice cream. ⓐ Via A Gramsci 4, Castel Gandolfo ⓣ 06 9360004 ⓦ www.pagnanelli.it 🕒 12.30–15.00, 19.30–23.00 Wed–Mon, closed Tues

ACCOMMODATION

Hotel Villa Maria Luigia £ A small, inexpensive hotel situated in its own private park. All rooms have modern amenities, and breakfast is included. ⓐ Via di Cisternole 204, Frascati ⓣ 06 9464430 ⓦ www.villamarialuigia.it

Hotel Castelvecchio ££ A luxury hotel with Art Nouveau interiors, five minutes' walk from the Papal Palace. There's a good on-site restaurant and a swimming pool. ⓐ Viale Pio XI 23, Castel Gandolfo ⓣ 06 9360308 ⓦ www.hotelcastelvecchio.com

◗ *The imposing Castello Orsini-Odescalchi in Bracciano*

PRACTICAL
information

Directory

GETTING THERE
By air
Budget airlines have made it possible to fly direct from the UK to Rome into Ciampino and Fiumicino from London Stansted and Luton, Glasgow Prestwick and East Midlands Airports.

Fares depend on which season you choose to travel. The highest are at Easter, any time between June through to mid-August and Christmas through to New Year. Weekend travel can add an extra 10 per cent to the round-trip fare, not including taxes and airport charges.

Airlines in the UK, Ireland & Italy
Aer Lingus ❶ UK 0845 084 4444; Republic of Ireland 0818 365 0000 Ⓦ www.aerlingus.com

Air Berlin ❶ UK 0870 738 8880 Ⓦ www.airberlin.com

Air Malta ❶ UK 0845 607 3710 Ⓦ www.airmalta.com

British Airways ❶ UK 0870 850 9850; Republic of Ireland 0800 616 747 Ⓦ www.britishairways.com

easyJet ❶ UK 0871 750 0100 Ⓦ www.easyjet.com

Meridiana ❶ UK 020 7730 3454 Ⓦ www.meridiana.it

Ryanair ❶ UK 0871 246 0000; Republic of Ireland 0818 303 030 Ⓦ www.ryanair.com

TUIfly ❶ UK 0870 606 0519 Ⓦ www.tuifly.com

Volare ❶ UK 0800 032 0992; outside UK +44 20 7365 8235 Ⓦ www.volareweb.com

Airlines in the US & Canada
Air Canada ❶ 1 888 247 2262 Ⓦ www.aircanada.ca

American Airlines ❶ 1 800 433 7300 Ⓦ www.aa.com

British Airways US & Canada 📞 1 800 AIRWAYS
🌐 www.britishairways.com
Delta Airlines 📞 1 800 241 4141 🌐 www.delta.com
Iberia 📞 1 800 772 4642 🌐 www.iberia.com
KLM/Northwest 📞 UK 0870 242 9242; US 1 800 447 4747
🌐 www.klm.com
Lufthansa 📞 UK 0870 837 7747; US 1 800 645 3880;
Canada 1 800 563 5954 🌐 www.lufthansa.com
SAS Scandinavian Airlines 📞 1 800 221 2350 🌐 www.flysas.com

Many people are aware that air travel emits CO_2, which contributes to climate change. You may be interested in the possibility of lessening the environmental impact of your flight through the charity **Climate Care**, which offsets your CO_2 by funding environmental projects around the world (visit 🌐 www.jpmorganclimatecare.com).

By rail
The Europe-wide InterRail and Eurail passes give unlimited travel on the Italian rail network.

Travelling by train to Rome is no less expensive than flying and the trip takes 16–18 hours from St Pancras International in London.

Eurail 🌐 www.eurail.com
Eurostar 📞 08705 186 186 🌐 www.eurostar.com
InterRail 🌐 www.interrailnet.com
Rail Europe 📞 08708 30 20 08 🌐 www.raileurope.co.uk

By road
This is not the recommended mode of travel unless you have a phobia of flying or trains, as it takes a gruelling 24 hours or even longer.

National Express Eurolines ℹ UK 08717 81 81 81, Ireland 01 836 6111
🅦 www.eurolines.co.uk

ENTRY FORMALITIES

British citizens need a valid passport to enter Italy. All other European Union (EU) citizens can enter the country by producing either a valid passport or a national identity card. All EU citizens may stay in the country for as long as they wish. Citizens of the United States, Canada, Australia and New Zealand need a valid passport, but are limited to stays of three months. All other nationals should consult the relevant embassies (see page 155) about requirements.

The amount of duty-free goods (bought in local shops) you can take from Italy varies according to whether you are going to an EU country or a non-EU country.

For the latest regulations visit 🅦 www.taxfreetravel.com or 🅦 www.hmrc.gov.uk/customs

In May 2005 a new legislation was introduced to crack down on the sellers and buyers of counterfeit items, such as purses, sunglasses, watches and belts. Criminal charges may be brought against people caught purchasing counterfeit products while in Italy. Fines can go up to a very hefty €10,000.

MONEY

Italy's currency is the euro, and notes are issued in denominations of 5, 10, 20, 50, 100, 200 and 500 euros. Coins are issued in denominations of 1, 2, 5, 10, 20 and 50 cents, and 1 and 2 euros.

It is a good idea to have some cash to hand when you first arrive. There are ATMs and money exchange bureaux at the airports, and many scattered throughout Rome. Check with your bank to make sure that your credit or debit card personal identification number gives you access to cashpoint machines (ATMs) abroad. The cards can be used at hotels, restaurants, some shops and for cash advances.

HEALTH, SAFETY & CRIME

The European Health Insurance Card (EHIC) – formerly the E111 form – is valid for five years. The Australian Medicare system also has a reciprocal healthcare agreement.

Vaccinations are not required, and Italy does not present any serious health worries. The worst that could possibly happen to you is sunstroke from extreme heat in summer or an upset stomach.

An Italian *farmacia* (pharmacist) is very qualified to give medical advice on minor ailments and to dispense prescriptions. There are generally one or more pharmacies, open 24 hours on a rotation basis, in each district in Rome. You can find the contact information on any pharmacy door or in the local newspaper.

Rome is generally a very safe city; petty crime, however, is rife. Gangs of *scippatori* (bag snatchers) strike in crowded streets, particularly on crowded buses or at major tourist sites. Whether on foot or riding scooters, they act fast, disappearing before you have even had time to react. It is not only handbags they are after; they can whip wallets out of your pocket, tear off visible jewellery and cameras, and can even undo a watch strap. Be vigilant and use your common sense when withdrawing money and carrying your bags.

In the event of theft, report it to the police, which in Rome is principally between the *Vigli Urbani*, who are mainly concerned with traffic and parking tickets, or the *Polizia Statale*, the main crime-fighting force. There is also the *Carabinieri*, who deal with general crime. All three have offices in Termini, the central train station. The central police station is off Via Nazionale at Via San Vitale 15 (contactable via **ⓘ** 06 46861).

OPENING HOURS

In general, opening hours are 09.30–13.00, 15.30–19.30 for shops and major chain and department stores. Family-owned and food businesses are closed on Sundays and Monday mornings; local food shops close on Thursday afternoons. The big department stores, fashion-chain stores and many of the shops in and around Via del Corso, Via del Tritone, Piazza di Spagna and the city centre stay open through lunch and do reduced hours on Sundays.

TOILETS

Train and bus stations are the best options, but facilities have improved around tourist sites in recent years. Most cafés and restaurants reserve use of facilities for patrons only. Toilets run the gamut from clean and modern to a hole in the floor. Have packets of sanitary wipes with you at all times.

CHILDREN

As elsewhere in family-oriented Italy, children are readily accepted in Rome. Indeed the city has gone to some considerable lengths over recent years to provide interesting attractions for the odd child who may not be a budding ancient historian: while sightseeing may bore very young children, you can keep them amused with plenty of alternative entertainments. The zoo at **Bioparco** at Villa Borghese (Ⓐ Via del Giordino Zoologico, Villa Borghese ❶ 06 3608211 Ⓦ www.bioparco.it) is a real child-pleaser. Indoor activities include **Time Elevator** (Ⓐ Via dei Santissimi Apostoli 20 ❶ 06 97746243 Ⓦ www.timeelevator.it), an amazing experience where flight-simulator seats and headphones give little ones (and their parents) a virtual tour of 3,000 years of Roman history. Then there's **Explora: Museo dei Bambini di Roma** (Ⓐ Via Flaminia 82 ❶ 06 3613776

Ⓦ www.mdbr.it), where children are encouraged to become aware of their place in the world – don't worry: it's loads of fun and nowhere near as earnest as it sounds. At the weekend the children can be entertained by an Italian puppet show on the Janiculum Hill. In Piazza Scanderbeg, close to the Trevi Fountain, is the **Museo Nazionale delle Paste Alimentari** (☏ 06 6991120 Ⓦ www.pastainmuseum.it), where you can learn all about the history of the famous Italian pasta. A quick look around will soon have the whole family drooling. Bowling, ice-skating, indoor rock climbing and roller-skating are all popular in Rome.

As far as food goes, Rome offers meals that generally appeal to kids, such as *gelato* (ice cream), pizza and spaghetti, and most restaurants will serve half-portions on request.

🔻 *Admire the fountains in the Piazza Navona*

COMMUNICATIONS

Internet

There is good Wi-Fi connection in Rome, with several outdoor Wi-Fi hotspots in lovely locations such as Villa Borghese, Piazza Navona and the Pantheon (for more info ⓦ www.romawireless.com). Internet terminals are easy to find, too. Hourly rates are €4–6. Make sure you have ID to hand, as it is now required before using the Internet in public Internet cafés due to new anti-terrorist legislation.

Mailboxes, Etc ⓐ Via del Gesù 91 (near the Pantheon) ⓣ 06 69190312 ⓛ 09.00–13.00, 14.00–18.30 Mon–Fri, 09.00–13.00 Sat, closed Sun

Museo del Corso ⓐ Via del Corso 320 ⓣ 06 6786209 ⓛ 10.00–18.00 Mon, 10.00–20.00 Tues–Thur & Sun, 10.00–22.00 Fri & Sat

Phone

Coin-operated telephones are almost extinct in Rome. It is best to purchase a *carta* or *scheda telefonica* (telephone card), available at *tabacchi* and newsstands. The telephone code for Rome is 06, which must be dialled before any Roman number, even if calling in Rome. Numbers with 800 are free, and dialling 170 gets you an English-speaking operator. Dial 176 for international directory enquiries. The phone tariffs are expensive, but there is a reduced rate for off-peak calls.

Post

The **main post office** in Rome (ⓛ 08.30–19.00 Mon–Fri, 08.00–13.15 Sat) is on Piazza San Silvestro 19. Other post offices open ⓛ 08.30–14.00 Mon–Fri, 08.00–13.00 Sat. *Francobolli* (stamps) can be purchased in *tabacchi*.

Central post offices

ⓐ Via Terme di Diocleziano 30 (Piazza Repubblica)

ⓐ Via Arenula 4 (Largo di Torre Argentina)
ⓐ Via Milano 18 (Via Nazionale)

ELECTRICITY

Electricity in Rome is 220 volts. Adaptors in Rome can be expensive, so it's best to try to bring one with you.

TRAVELLERS WITH DISABILITIES

The Vatican Museums and St Peter's, the Palatine and the Galleria Borghese are all accessible by wheelchair, but in general Rome with its cobbled streets, crowded pavements and chaotic traffic is not well organised for people with disabilities. Ramps, lifts and modified WCs exist in many museums and transport hubs, including Termini Station, and the situation is improving all the

TELEPHONING ITALY

From the UK, Ireland and New Zealand dial the access code 00 (011 from the USA and Canada, or 0011 from Australia), followed by the code for Italy (39), then the local number (including the 06 code).

TELEPHONING ABROAD

UK and Northern Ireland international access code 0044 + area code
Republic of Ireland international access code 00353 + area code
US & Canada international access code 001 + area code
Australia international access code 0061 + area code
New Zealand international access code 0064 + area code

time. Unescorted travellers with disabilities should consider package tours.

Handy Turismo is a service for disabled tourists to Rome (funded by Rome city council) and contains very useful information on monuments, hotels and restaurants with disabled access.

☎ 06 35075707 ⓦ www.handyturismo.it (in English and Italian)

For information regarding public transport for the disabled call ATAC's freephone number: ☎ 800 154451

⬤ *The postboxes are blue in the Vatican City*

TOURIST INFORMATION

Turismoroma (Ⓦ www.turismoroma.it), the Rome Tourist Board, provides information about Rome, hotel reservations, maps, and a very useful free monthly booklet called *Un Ospite a Roma* (Ⓦ www.aguestinrome.com) that contains cultural listings and information.

Tourist information booths are located in the arrivals section of Fiumicino Airport, and opposite platform 24 at Termini Station. Information kiosks are sprinkled throughout the city at visible locations. They are generally open 🕐 09.30–17.00

The city council also operates a tourist information call centre 📞 06 0608 🕐 daily 09.00–21.00, and an extremely comprehensive website at Ⓦ www.060608.it (also in English).

The friendly, English-speaking staff at **Enjoy Rome** (📍 Via Marghera 8a 📞 06 4451843 Ⓦ www.enjoyrome.com) offer a free room-finding service, tours and shuttle buses to the airport. They also provide maps and brochures, and advise where to eat, drink and go out.

Roma Pass The city of Rome offers a pass good for three days of public transport plus free admission to two museums, reduced prices for all other museums and major events and, alluringly, a dedicated entrance at the Colosseum. The cost of the three-day pass is €25. Buy them at tourist kiosks, museum ticket counters or online. Ⓦ www.romapass.it

BACKGROUND READING

I, Claudius and *Claudius the God* by Robert Graves. The most evocative of the novels about the characters who shaped imperial Rome. *Rome: The Biography of a City* by Christopher Hibbert. A compelling account of the city's development.

Emergencies

EMERGENCY NUMBERS
Police ☎ 113, **Carabinieri** ☎ 112, **Fire** ☎ 115, **Ambulance** ☎ 118
Car breakdown (Automobile Club d'Italia) ☎ 803116

MEDICAL SERVICES
Consult the Yellow Pages under *medico*. If you need urgent medical care, go to the *pronto soccorso* (casualty department). All the hospitals listed below offer 24-hour casualty services.

Ospedale Fatebenefratelli 📍 Isola Tiberina, Ghetto ☎ 06 68371 🚌 Bus: H, 23, 63, 280, 630, 780; Tram: 8

Ospedale Pediatrico Bambino Gesù (Children's Hospital) 📍 Piazza Sant'Onofrio 4, Gianicolo ☎ 06 68591 🚌 Bus: 115, 870

Ospedale San Camillo-Forlanini 📍 Via Portuense 332, Suburbs; west ☎ 06 55551/06 58701 🚌 Bus: H, 228, 710, 719, 773, 774, 786, 791; Tram: 8

Ospedale San Giacomo 📍 Via Canova 29, Tridente ☎ 06 36261 or ☎ 06 3227069 🚌 Bus: 117, 119, 590; Metro: Spagna

Ospedale San Giovanni 📍 Via dell'Amba Aradam 8, San Giovanni ☎ 06 77051 🚌 Bus: 81, 117, 650, 673, 714; Metro: San Giovanni

Policlinico Umberto I 📍 Viale del Policlinico 155, Suburbs; north ☎ 06 49971 🚌 Bus: 61, 310, 490, 491, 495, 649; Tram: 3, 19; Metro: Policlinico

Pharmacies
Farmacie (pharmacies) are identified by a green cross. Along with dispensing prescriptions, Italian pharmacists are well qualified to give informal medical advice on minor ailments. Make sure you know the generic as well as the brand name of your regular medicines, as they may be sold under a different name in Italy. Normal opening hours for pharmacies are ⏰ 08.30–13.30, 16.30–20.00 Mon–Fri. Outside these

hours a duty rota system operates. A list by the door of any pharmacy and in local newspapers indicates the nearest one open at any time.

The following chemists are open 24 hours a day:

Farmacia Senato (near Piazza Navona) Corso Rinascimento 50 🛈 06 68803760 Ⓝ Bus: 30, 40, 46, 62, 64, 70, 81, 87, 116, 492, 571, 628, 916

Farmacia della Stazione Ⓐ Piazza dei Cinquecento 49–51 🛈 06 4880019 Ⓝ Bus: H, 16, 36, 38, 40; Tram: 5, 14; Metro: Termini

Piram Ⓐ Via Nazionale 228 🛈 06 4880754 Ⓝ Bus: H, 40; Metro: Repubblica

EMBASSIES & CONSULATES

Australia Ⓐ Via Antonio Bosio 5 🛈 06 852721

Canada Ⓐ Via Salaria 243 🛈 06 854441

Republic of Ireland Ⓐ Piazza Campitelli 3 🛈 06 6979121

New Zealand Ⓐ Via Clitunno 44 🛈 06 8537501

UK Ⓐ Via XX Settembre 80a 🛈 06 42200001

US Ⓐ Via Veneto 119a 🛈 06 46741

EMERGENCY PHRASES

Help!	**Fire!**	**Stop!**
Aiuto!	Fuoco!	Fermi!
Ahyootoh!	*Fwohkoh!*	*Fehrmee!*

Call an ambulance/a doctor/the police/the fire service!
Chiami un'ambulanza/un medico/la polizia/i pompieri!
Kyahmee oon ahmboolahntsa/oon mehdeecoh/
lah pohleetseeyah/ee pohmpyehree!

ACKNOWLEDGEMENTS

The publishers would like to thank the following individuals and organisations for supplying their copyright photographs for this book: Alamy Ltd Martin Belam page 31; Dreamstime (Chiara Lozzi) page 7; Pado Cipriani page 45; Stefaniav page 57; Ritami Annuar page 87; Antoine Beyeleri page 91; Monica Boorboor page 92;Timehacker page 104; Fefoff page 106; Asier Villafranca page 112; Alfredo Rogazzonio page 137; Marini1957 page 143; Giovanna Dunmall pages 83 & 95; Kim S page 152; Jon Smith page 70; World Pictures/Photoshot pages 25, 29 & 85; Christopher Holt, all others.

Project Editor: Jennifer Jahn
Layout: Paul Queripel
Proofreaders: Karolin Thomas & Jan McCann

Send your thoughts to
books@thomascook.com

- Found a great bar, club, shop or must-see sight that we don't feature?
- Like to tip us off about any information that needs a little updating?
- Want to tell us what you love about this handy little guidebook and more importantly how we can make it even handier?

Then here's your chance to tell all! Send us ideas, discoveries and recommendations today and then look out for your valuable input in the next edition of this title.

Email the above address (stating the title) or write to: pocket guides Series Editor, Thomas Cook Publishing, PO Box 227, Coningsby Road, Peterborough PE3 8SB, UK.

WHAT'S IN YOUR GUIDEBOOK?

Independent authors Impartial up-to-date information from our travel experts who meticulously source local knowledge.

Experience Thomas Cook's 165 years in the travel industry and guidebook publishing enriches every word with expertise you can trust.

Travel know-how Thomas Cook has thousands of staff working around the globe, all living and breathing travel.

Editors Travel-publishing professionals, pulling everything together to craft a perfect blend of words, pictures, maps and design.

You, the traveller We deliver a practical, no-nonsense approach to information, geared to how you really use it.

Useful phrases

English	Italian	Approx pronunciation
BASICS		
Yes	Sì	*See*
No	No	*Noh*
Please	Per favore	*Pehr fahvohreh*
Thank you	Grazie	*Grahtsyeh*
Hello	Buongiorno/Ciao	*Bwonjohrnoh/Chow*
Goodbye	Arrivederci/Ciao	*Ahreevehderchee/Chow*
Excuse me	Scusi	*Skoozee*
Sorry	Mi dispiace	*Mee deespyahcheh*
That's okay	Va bene	*Vah behneh*
I don't speak Italian	Non parlo italiano	*Non pahrloh eetahlyahnoh*
Do you speak English?	Parla inglese?	*Pahrlah eenglehzeh?*
Good morning	Buongiorno	*Bwonjohrnoh*
Good afternoon	Buon pomeriggio	*Bwon pohmehreejoh*
Good evening	Buona sera	*Bwonah sehrah*
Goodnight	Buona notte	*Bwonah nohteh*
My name is ...	Mi chiamo ...	*Mee kyahmoh ...*
NUMBERS		
One	Uno	*Oonoh*
Two	Due	*Dooeh*
Three	Tre	*Treh*
Four	Quattro	*Kwahttroh*
Five	Cinque	*Cheenkweh*
Six	Sei	*Say*
Seven	Sette	*Sehteh*
Eight	Otto	*Ohtoh*
Nine	Nove	*Nohveh*
Ten	Dieci	*Dyehchee*
Twenty	Venti	*Ventee*
Fifty	Cinquanta	*Cheenkwahntah*
One hundred	Cento	*Chentoh*
SIGNS & NOTICES		
Airport	Aeroporto	*Ahehrohpohrtoh*
Railway station	Stazione ferroviaria	*Stahtsyoneh fehrohveeahreeah*
Platform	Binario	*Beenahreeyoh*
Smoking/non-smoking	Fumatori/non fumatori	*Foomahtohree/non foomahtohree*
Toilets	Bagni	*Bahnyee*
Ladies/Gentlemen	Signore/Signori	*Seenyoreh/Seenyohree*
Subway	Metropolitana	*Mehtrohpohleetahnah*